Y0-BZA-848

megiddo 1918

lawrence, allenby, and the march on damascus

BRYAN PERRETT

megiddo 1918

lawrence, allenby, and the march on damascus

Praeger Illustrated Military History Series

PRAEGER

Westport, Connecticut
London

Library of Congress Cataloging-in-Publication Data

Perrett, Bryan.
    Megiddo 1918 : Lawrence, Allenby, and the march on Damascus / Bryan Perrett.
       p. cm – (Praeger illustrated military history, ISSN 1547-206X)
    Originally published: Oxford: Osprey, 1999.
    Includes bibliographical references and index.
    ISBN 0-275-98292-0 (alk. paper)
    1. Megiddo, Battle of, Israel, 1918. 2. Lawrence, T. E. (Thomas Edward), 1888-1935.
    3. Allenby, Edmund Henry Hynman Allenby, Viscount, 1861–1936. 4. Damascus (Syria)
    – History, Military – 20th century. I. Title. II. Series.
    D568.7.P47 2004
    940.4'38–dc22   2003064186

British Library Cataloguing in Publication Data is available.

First published in paperback in 1999 by Osprey Publishing Limited, Elms Court,
Chapel Way, Botley, Oxford OX2 9LP. All rights reserved.

Copyright © 2004 by Osprey Publishing Limited

All rights reserved. No portion of this book may be reproduced, by any process
or technique, without the express written consent of the publisher.

Library of Congress Catalog Card Number: 2003064186
ISBN: 0-275-98292-0
ISSN: 1547-206X

Praeger Publishers, 88 Post Road West, Westport, CT 06881
An imprint of Greenwood Publishing Group, Inc.
www.praeger.com

Printed in China through World Print Ltd.

The paper used in this book complies with the Permanent Paper Standard issued
by the National Information Standards Organization (Z39.48-1984).

10 9 8 7 6 5 4 3 2 1

ILLUSTRATED BY: Ed Dovey

CONTENTS

Key to military series symbols

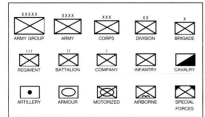

ORIGINS OF
THE CAMPAIGN

Following Turkey's entry into the Great War on the side of the Central Powers, British strategy in the Middle East called for the re-opening of warm-water communications with Russia by forcing the Dardanelles, the occupation of Basra to secure the Mesopotamian oil fields, and a defensive stance in Egypt. The first of these ventures was an unmitigated disaster. The second, though ultimately successful, became prematurely over-extended and was punctuated by the siege and surrender of General Townshend's force at Kut-al-Amara. The third alone achieved its objective, although even here there were moments which gave rise to serious anxiety.

Although the Sinai desert offered the defenders of the Suez Canal some protection, the canal could be crossed by an army, provided adequate logistic preparations had been made. In this respect the Turks were at something of a disadvantage, since their coastal shipping had been brought to a standstill by the Allied navies. Furthermore, their rail supply route was awkwardly constructed, and since it had a great bearing on subsequent operations it is worth describing in some detail.

In theory, a standard-gauge single-track line ran all the way from the Bosphorus through Asia Minor to Muslimiya Junction, where a branch left for Mesopotamia while the main line continued south into Syria as far as Riyaq. In fact, the line was broken by two long uncompleted sections in

In the vast spaces of the Middle Eastern theatre of war, mechanised units often played a critical role. Shown here is one of the original Rolls-Royce vehicles of the Duke of Westminster's armoured car brigade, which was employed with great success against the Senussi. Note the planks for use as rudimentary sand channels, tow rope, jack and tyre levers, all very necessary items in the sort of going encountered. (Trustees of the Imperial War Museum Negative Q15725)

Motorcyclists and Model T Fords of a Light Car Patrol, photographed near El Alamein After the defeat of the Senussi. Light Car Patrols became responsible for policing the Western Desert. The topographical information they supplied was also put to good use during World War II. (IWM)

the Taurus and Amanus mountains, where troops and supplies had to detour by road. At Riyaq the line became narrow-gauge, and the next stage of the journey could either be along a branch that crossed the mountains to Beirut, or down the main line to Damascus and then to Deraa. There it forked again, with one branch running to El Auja, near Beersheba, with connections to Haifa, Jaffa and Jerusalem, and the other – the famous Hejaz or Pilgrim railway – going straight down through Arabia to Medina.

The operation of the rail system was difficult at best, since the war denied Turkey much of her locomotive coal and wood could only be obtained by felling sparse local timber; ultimately the Turks were forced to use anything that would burn, including dried camel dung. Again, a narrow-gauge single-track system could not hope to keep pace with the demands of a modern army in the field, and even with the generous assistance of animal transport, there was a ceiling on the number of troops that could be physically supported beyond the railheads.

Nevertheless, at the beginning of January 1915 the Turkish commanders in southern Palestine planned a raid against the Suez Canal, hoping to damage installations and disrupt traffic with sunken blockships. The troops detailed for the operation were the Turkish VIII Corps, commanded by Djemal Bey, whose team of German advisers was led by Colonel Freiherr Kress von Kressenstein. By the middle of January the corps was ready to leave Beersheba and embark on its crossing of the Sinai, which had been evacuated by the British the previous autumn. The coastal route was to be avoided since it would have brought the marching columns within range of naval gunfire. Fortunately the inland route, though hot and arid in summer, was now quite passable because heavy winter rains had filled the pools and cisterns along the way. Nevertheless, 5,000 water-carrying camels were required to prevent thirst becoming an acute problem.

The British had been expecting the Turkish advance, and its progress was reported by Nieuport seaplanes flying off the canal. This gave the defenders plenty of time to prepare. On 3 February the Turks launched a series of uncoordinated attacks along a wide front. They were defeated in

detail. Djemal retired slowly to Beersheba, having incurred some 2,000 casualties to no purpose. British casualties amounted to only 163, but no pursuit was attempted since it was impossible to venture far into the Sinai without adequate preparation.

The Turks next attempted to cause trouble for the British in Egypt by stirring up the warlike Senussi Muslim sect. The Senussi lived mainly in Libya and, never having accepted the fact that since the war between Italy and Turkey in 1912 the province had become an Italian colony, they were engaged in a guerrilla war against the newcomers, confining them to a narrow coastal strip. The Sultan now called for a *jihad* (holy war) against all foreigners, including the British. Having supplied the Senussi with artillery, machine guns, ammunition and advisers, the Sultan had them landed by submarine on deserted stretches of the Libyan coast, and urged them to invade Egypt, pointing to the repulse of the Gallipoli landings as a sign of British weakness. He promised that Senussi supporters would rise and complete the destruction of the Infidel. Thus encouraged, the Senussi crossed the frontier on 17 November 1915.

Lieutenant-general Sir John Maxwell, responsible for the security of Egypt, had very few troops available, and this latest threat was contained only with difficulty. The arrival of reinforcements and troops back from Gallipoli tipped the scale, however, and after several hard-fought actions the Senussi were pushed back into Libya.

Operations against the Senussi would continue until February 1917. During these, the armoured cars of the Light Armoured Motor Batteries (LAMBs) and open Fords of the Light Car Patrols proved to be the most effective weapons in the British armoury, since they were capable of independent action in the vast spaces of the western desert.

If the Turkish attempt to create a running sore for the British in this area was to prove a failure, the reverse was true of British efforts to return the compliment in Arabia. Here the Arab tribes, led by Sherif Abdullah and his son, the Emir Feisal, broke out in full-scale revolt against the

The busy marshalling yard of the Trans-Sinai Railway at El Kantara on the east bank of the Suez Canal. Murray's advance across Sinai and Allenby's subsequent campaign in Palestine depended upon sound logistic planning. (Museum of Army Transport)

Ottoman Empire in June 1916, capturing Mecca and besieging the Turkish garrison at Medina. British military aid began to flow at once, accompanied by a team of advisers, of whom the best remembered was the then Captain T. E. Lawrence.

Military common sense dictated that Medina was economically untenable, but as honour was involved, the Turks decided to hold the city. To do so required the movement of supplies and reinforcements along the Hejaz railway, and here they were at their most vulnerable. Lawrence, who later gained in stature and rank following the capture of the port of Aqaba in June 1917, saw the Turkish weakness and decided to exploit it. His policy was to allow the railway to function, but only just. His raids suited the Arab temperament and kept thousands of Turkish troops uselessly pinned down in garrisons and blockhouses.

Important diversions as they were, neither the Senussi war nor the Arab revolt could resolve the trans-Sinai stand-off. After Gallipoli the now considerable British military presence in Egypt was formed into an Egyptian Expeditionary Force under Lieutenant-general Sir Archibald Murray, who had recently held the post of Chief of the Imperial General Staff. Officially, British strategic policy was still defensive. However, stung by Kitchener's taunt – 'Are you defending the Canal or is it defending you?' – Murray was forced to think along more aggressive lines.

Having calculated that a renewed Turkish advance would enter Sinai through El Arish or El Kusseima, Murray decided to establish a 50-mile front between these two points. Yet even before this modest objective could be secured, much logistic groundwork had to be done; in this Murray was nothing if not thorough. Thousands of local labourers were engaged in constructing a standard-gauge railway from El Kantara on the canal. The railhead advanced across the Sinai at the rate of 50 miles per month, and in parallel a fresh-water pipeline was laid, complete with storage tanks, a portable reservoir, which could hold 500,000 gallons, and batteries of standpipes. Beyond the railhead an efficient camel transport corps supplied the forward troops.

Major-general Harry Chauvel (centre) and the Staff of the ANZAC Mounted Division. A regular officer of the Australian Army, Chauvel commanded the Desert Mounted Corps at Megiddo and is frequently referred to as the finest cavalry leader of modern times. (IWM Neg Q15777)

A Royal Horse Artillery battery
of the Yeomanry Division
crossing the Sinai. The advance
was made with the infantry
divisions closest to the coast
and the mounted troops covering
the open desert flank.
(IWM Neg Q50855)

This slow, methodical advance across the Sinai was made with the British infantry divisions close to the coast and the railhead, and the cavalry covering the open desert flank. The latter, commanded by the then Major-general Harry Chauvel, consisted of the Australian Mounted Division, the ANZAC Mounted Division, the British Yeomanry Division and a camel corps recruited mainly from the Australian Light Horse. The camel corps usually occupied the space between the marching infantry divisions and the mounted troops.

Kress von Kressenstein, now effectively commander of the Turkish Sinai sector, was well aware of what was going on. To him the British advance looked more like preparations for an offensive than the extension of a strategic defence. He decided to mount a spoiling attack on the railhead, which had now reached Romani, with 18,000 men, mainly good quality Anatolian troops, including many Gallipoli veterans. This took place on 3 August 1916 and was a fiercely contested action. Once the Turks' initial assault had been blunted by the 52nd (Lowland) Division, Chauvel's light horsemen moved in to counter-attack from the south-west. Kressenstein was forced to withdraw, having sustained 5,000 battle casualties and 4,000 men taken prisoner; British casualties amounted to little more than 1,000.

On 21 December the Turks were found to have abandoned El Arish. Two days later Chauvel's troopers stormed a strong position at Maghdaba, 20 miles up the Wadi El Arish, and Murray had acquired the baseline for the strategic defence of Egypt. On 9 January 1917 the Turks were ejected from Magruntein, 25 miles beyond El Arish and just south of Rafah, their last toe-hold in Egypt.

The course of the campaign was now influenced by high-level politics. One faction in the British war cabinet, the 'Westerners', adhered to the conventional military wisdom that the Central Powers could only be defeated by overcoming the main mass of their strength,

British infantry on the march. If the men seem small and even scrawny by today's standards, this was balanced by extreme mental and physical toughness. (IWM Neg Q24374)

which was deployed along the Western Front. The other, the 'Easterners', led by Prime Minister Lloyd George, believed that the elimination of Turkey, the weakest member of the enemy alliance, would have a domino effect and be followed in turn by the collapse of Bulgaria, Austria-Hungary and Germany. The Chief of the Imperial General Staff, General Sir William Robertson, was not altogether convinced by the Easterners' argument but, partly because he was opposed to a fresh offensive on the Western Front and partly because Murray seemed to be doing well, he approved a plan for a limited offensive which, it was hoped, would result in the capture of Gaza.

Murray waited until his railhead had caught up and launched his attack on 26 March 1917. However, defective staff work resulted in troops being withdrawn from vital ground at the very moment the German garrison commander was considering surrender, and the attack failed, with heavy casualties. Unwisely Murray's despatches struck a dishonestly optimistic note, claiming that the operation 'just fell short of a complete disaster to the enemy'.

The Arab revolt against the Ottoman Empire received immediate British support. Here, a team of advisers is encamped round a well-head in an Arabian wadi. The cut-down tender in the foreground was previously one of the Duke of Westminster's armoured cars and was frequently used by the then Captain T. E. Lawrence. (IWM Neg Q59573)

Kressenstein's reaction was to turn Gaza into a fortress and create a defensive line stretching inland to Beersheba. On 17 April Murray tried again, using the 52nd (Lowland), 53rd (Welsh) and 54th (East Anglian) divisions, reinforced with a small detachment of tanks. Unfortunately the tanks were squandered in penny packets and the Second Battle of Gaza also ended in a decisive repulse, with even heavier British casualties. This time there could be no concealing failure. Murray, a capable and intelligent officer who had brought his army across Sinai in good order, had fallen victim to his own vanity and so was dismissed.

Murray's successor, General Sir Edmund Allenby, received reinforcements from the Salonika front and the Aden garrison. His army now consisted of three corps: the Desert Mounted Corps, XX Corps with four infantry divisions and XXI Corps with three infantry divisions. In Mesopotamia General Maude's army had captured Baghdad in March, and Lloyd George told Allenby that he wanted Jerusalem as a Christmas present. Allenby therefore began planning what became known as the Third Battle of Gaza/Beersheba. The plan involved the Desert Mounted Corps seizing Beersheba by *coup de main* while XXI Corps mounted a strong feint attack on Gaza. XX Corps would then roll up the unhinged Turkish line from the east.

In the event, the results exceeded Allenby's expectations. Beersheba fell to a dashing attack by the Australian and ANZAC Mounted Divisions on 31 October, and the next day XXI Corps' feint attack, made with the entire tank detachment concentrated under 54th Division, actually broke through the defences at Gaza. Allenby promptly reinforced this unexpected success and the Turks began retreating northwards. They attempted holding actions at Huj on 8 November and at El Maghar on 13 November, but on both occasions spirited actions by yeomanry overran their rearguards. On 14 November armoured cars of 12th LAMB charged into Junction Station, where the Jerusalem branch met the enemy's main railway line. The pursuit ended on 16 November with the capture of Jaffa by the ANZAC Mounted Division. Most of the British infantry divisions were now involved in heavy fighting in the Judean hills. The Turks managed to slow the pace of the advance but failed to halt it. By the morning of 9 December the last Turkish garrison had abandoned Jerusalem.

Turkish infantry and machine gunners manning trenches near Beersheba. Barbed wire has been strung beyond grenade-throwing distance but was in short supply in the Middle East and its depth never approached that of the fearsome entanglements on the Western Front. (Dr David Nicolle)

Turkish anti-aircraft gunners and German instructors at Beersheba. Note the circular gun platform and the rangefinder. (Bundesarchiv Neg 70/73/29)

The price of Allenby's 1917 offensive was 18,000 casualties, but the Turks had lost 25,000 men and their morale was seriously shaken. Kressenstein was replaced by General Erich von Falkenhayn, a former Chief of German General Staff and the conqueror of Romania the previous year. In fighting to the north of the city he managed to re-establish something like a coherent defence. Further operations were brought to a standstill by the heaviest rains in living memory, the lines eventually stretching from the sea to the Jordan valley.

Whatever Allenby's plans might have been for the spring of 1918, they were overtaken by events. On the Western Front Ludendorff's series of offensives came close to breaking the Allied line, and Allenby was required to send almost three-quarters of his experienced British infantry battalions and yeomanry regiments, together with an appropriate number of artillery and machine gun units, to restore the manpower crisis that had developed in France. By degrees these gaps were made good with Indian and other troops, only some of whom were experienced, but during the spring and early summer months Allenby was forced to remain on the defensive; significantly, although they must have been aware of the situation, neither Falkenhayn nor his successor, Liman von Sanders, made any attempt to exploit the temporary British weakness.

In March and April Allenby launched two raids across the Jordan at Amman, both of which met with stiff opposition and were forced back. However, the raids did attract enemy formations which would otherwise have been available to contest the advance of the Arab army from the south. As the summer drew on, the strength of Allenby's own army was progressively increased until he was able to plan the battle that would end the campaign.

THE THIRD BATTLE OF GAZA/BEERSHEBA

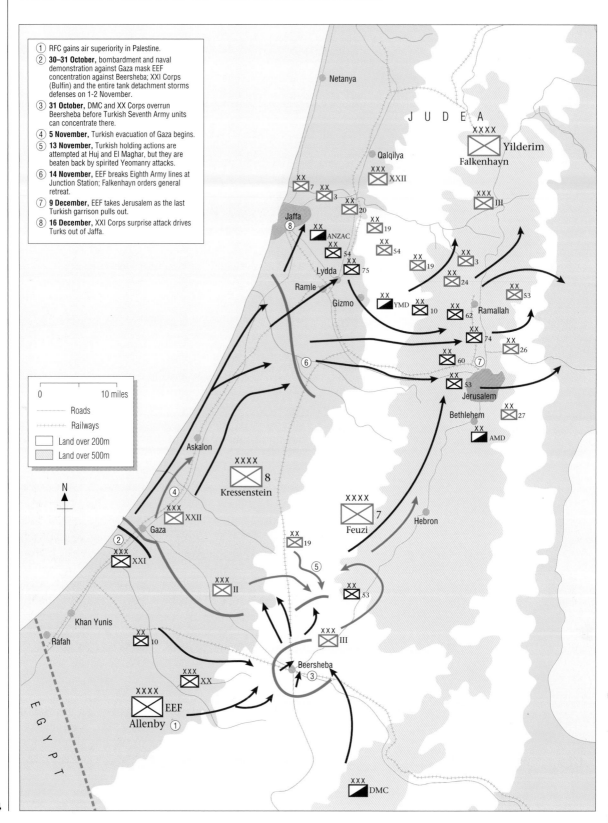

1. RFC gains air superiority in Palestine.
2. **30–31 October,** bombardment and naval demonstration against Gaza mask EEF concentration against Beersheba; XXI Corps (Bulfin) and the entire tank detachment storms defenses on 1-2 November.
3. **31 October,** DMC and XX Corps overrun Beersheba before Turkish Seventh Army units can concentrate there.
4. **5 November,** Turkish evacuation of Gaza begins.
5. **13 November,** Turkish holding actions are attempted at Huj and El Maghar, but they are beaten back by spirited Yeomanry attacks.
6. **14 November,** EEF breaks Eighth Army lines at Junction Station; Falkenhayn orders general retreat.
7. **9 December,** EEF takes Jerusalem as the last Turkish garrison pulls out.
8. **16 December,** XXI Corps surprise attack drives Turks out of Jaffa.

Netanya

J U D E A

Qalqilya

Yilderim
Falkenhayn

Jaffa

XXII

III

ANZAC

54

Lydda

75

Ramle

Gizmo

YMD

Ramallah

62

10

53

19

54

19

3

24

74

26

60

7

Jerusalem

Bethlehem

53

27

AMD

0   10 miles

Roads
Railways
Land over 200m
Land over 500m

Askalon

N

Kressenstein

8

Gaza

XXII

XXI

7
Feuzi

Hebron

Khan Yunis

Rafah

10

XX

II

19

5

53

III

Beersheba

EEF
Allenby

DMC

E G Y P T

14

OPPOSING COMMANDERS

THE ALLIES

General Sir Edmund Allenby (1861–1936)

A former Inspector General of Cavalry, Allenby had commanded the Cavalry Division of the British Expeditionary Force in 1914. He was appointed commander of the Third Army in October 1915 and handled it competently during the Battle of Arras in 1917. However, he shared a mutual antipathy with Haig, and when Murray failed at Second Gaza he was appointed to succeed him as Commander-in-Chief Egypt in June 1917. Known as 'The Bull', partly because of his build and partly because he was inclined to bellow when enraged, Allenby's first act on arrival was to move GHQ from the comforts of Cairo to a position much closer to the front so that he would become a familiar figure to his troops. During Third Gaza/Beersheba, 31 October 1917, he demonstrated his tactical flexibility by exploiting the success of what had originally been intended as a feint attack at the western end of the line.

To the Palestinian Arabs Allenby became an almost mystical figure, not only because their pronunciation of his name – *'Allah en Nebi'* – could only be translated as 'the prophet of God', but also because, having captured Jerusalem on 9 December, he chose, either by inclination or as a matter of policy, to enter the Holy City humbly and on foot, thereby fulfilling an ancient prophecy to the effect that a saviour from the West would do so and free them from Turkish rule.

Allenby could probably have finished off the Turkish army in Palestine during the spring of 1918 had he not been forced to send many of his experienced units to France to counter German offensives on the Western Front. Once the situation there had been brought under control he was himself reinforced, mainly with Indian troops, and was able

General Sir Edmund Allenby, perhaps the best British general of World War I.
(IWM Neg Q82969)

15

to plan Megiddo. His recognition that once the front had been broken deep penetration could be used to destroy the enemy's command and logistic infrastructure won him the battle and was a major milestone on the road to developing what became known as the *blitzkrieg* technique.

Like many great commanders, including Montgomery, Allenby could be utterly ruthless with subordinates who failed at critical moments. Field marshal Earl Wavell, who served on his staff, believed that he was the best British general of World War I. After the campaign's sudden and dramatic end Allenby was promoted to field marshal and created Viscount Allenby of Megiddo. He subsequently served as the British High Commissioner in Egypt, virtually ruling the country until it achieved its independence.

THE CENTRAL POWERS

General Otto Liman von Sanders (1855–1929)

Of Jewish descent, Liman was ennobled in July 1913, after which he adopted the maiden name of his late wife, a Scot, to complement the honorific 'von'. He was one of the most senior divisional commanders in the German army at the time, and while promotion was due, in the harsh opinion of General Hans von Seeckt, the future architect of the Reichsheer, it was doubts concerning Liman's ability to command a German corps that resulted in his appointment as leader of the German Military Mission to the Ottoman Empire in December 1913.

Liman's task of modernising the Turkish army was complicated by disagreements with the German ambassador and by the indolence of

Tanks were used in small numbers during the Second and Third Battles of Gaza, breaking the enemy front on the latter occasion. The Tank Detachment was withdrawn in 1918 to meet the crisis developinq on the Western Front, and none were available for Megiddo. (RAC Tank Museum Neg 102.50.10)

General Otto Liman von Sanders allowed his successful defence of the Gallipoli peninsula to influence him unduly in Palestine. (Bundesarchiv Neg 70/60/24)

Turkish ministers, who frustrated his efforts to such an extent that he seriously considered challenging two of them to a duel. How all this might have ended there is no telling, for on the outbreak of war in August 1914 he was appointed commander of the Turkish First Army. The following year he became commander of the Turkish Fifth Army, with which he successfully contained the Allied landings on the Gallipoli peninsula. Here, although he made tactical errors of judgement, he displayed qualities of stubbornness that ultimately compelled the Allies to abandon this costly and abortive venture.

In February 1918 Liman was appointed commander of the Palestine Front, replacing the defeated General Erich von Falkenhayn, whose advice he declined to accept. His unenviable situation was further complicated by the refusal of Enver Pasha, the Turkish war minister, and Von Seeckt, the Turkish army's chief of staff since the previous December, to supply the resources he felt he needed.

Liman von Sanders had only two things in common with his opponent Allenby; both were cavalrymen and neither would tolerate inefficiency in subordinates. In other respects their outlooks were completely opposed, for while Allenby remained an apostle of mobility, Sanders, conditioned by his experience at Gallipoli, was now a convert to the theory of holding ground at any price, forgetting that in Palestine ground was of infinitely less value than in the Dardanelles. Nevertheless, he did his best with the resources available to him. His greatest faults as a commander were, perhaps, a lack of imagination coupled with an inability to recognise terrain of critical importance. His active career ended when Turkey concluded an armistice with the Allies.

THE OPPOSING ARMIES

THE ALLIED ARMY

Allenby's army at Megiddo was very different from that with which he had won Third Gaza/Beersheba the previous year. With many of his British units in France to counter German offensives on the Western Front, by September the Egyptian Expeditionary Force was imperial in character and much of it was organised on Indian army lines. Among some more inexperienced Indian units were the Guides and Frontier Force regiments, regarded as an elite.

Most of the cavalry were concentrated in Lieutenant-general Sir Harry Chauvel's Desert Mounted Corps, which retained its title even though the Sinai Desert had long been left behind. Initially Chauvel's command had included a camel corps, but this had now been disbanded and its men returned to their parent units.

The Desert Mounted Corps consisted of the 4th and 5th Cavalry Divisions, the Australian and New Zealand (ANZAC) Mounted Division, which was detached for the Megiddo operation, and the Australian Mounted Division. Both cavalry divisions' order of battle followed that of the Indian army and reflected the lessons learned during the Great Mutiny the previous century. Each brigade contained one British regiment, with yeomanry substituted for the usual regular units, and within the Indian regiments each sabre squadron was recruited from a different martial race. Most of the Indian troopers were accustomed to professional soldiering in hard climates.

The ANZAC and Australian Mounted divisions consisted of Australian Light Horse or New Zealand Mounted Rifle regiments trained

Australian Light Horsemen encamped outside Damascus towards the end of the campaign. While their informal code of discipline may have alarmed British senior officers, they were truly formidable soldiers. (IWM Neg Q12355)

Gloucestershire Yeomanry
passing through Damascus.
The Yeomanry regiments
maintained their traditional
smartness throughout the
campaign, but were more
flexible in their approach than
their regular counterparts.
(IWM Neg Q12386)

to fight a fast-moving mounted infantry battle. Physically tough, aggressive, very experienced and natural hard riders, they were mounted on large, hardy, Australian horses known as 'Walers', a breed that stood up to the demanding climate better than any other. Their discipline was notoriously informal, but none the less effective, and they possessed a high level of personal initiative.

Like the British yeomanry regiments, they were more flexible in their approach than their regular counterparts; for example, after the previous year's experience, at its own request the Australian Mounted Division was trained with the sword. Also serving with the latter was a regiment of French Chasseurs d'Afrique, who performed well in action although their North African Arab and Barb mounts had difficulty keeping up with the big Walers of the Australian brigade. Operating as corps troops within the Desert Mounted Corps were two Light Armoured Motor Batteries equipped with Rolls Royce armoured cars and two Light Car Patrols equipped with unarmoured Model T Fords mounting Lewis light machine guns.

Within Allenby's two infantry corps, XX and XXI, as shown by their Order of Battle, only the 54th (East Anglian) Division retained its purely British and largely Territorial composition. Elements of the 10th, 53rd, 60th and 75th divisions revealed their respective Irish, Welsh, London and West Country origins but they were now essentially Indian divisions with one British battalion in each brigade. The companies of each Indian infantry battalion, unlike their cavalry equivalents, were all recruited from the same martial race.

The Imperial nature of the troops under Allenby's command was further emphasised by the presence of two battalions of the British West Indies Regiment, a South African field artillery brigade and a mountain battery recruited in Hong Kong and Singapore. In addition, the 38th and 39th battalions Royal Fusiliers were raised from Palestinian volunteers.

Allenby's artillery at Megiddo was flexibly handled, and achieved an overwhelming concentration of force on the sector chosen for the breakthrough. Its composition is contained in the Order of Battle. Below are set out some details of the performance of its principal weapons.

Type	Weight of shell (lb)	Range (yards)
13-pdr. gun	12	5,900
18-pdr. gun	18	7,000
60-pdr. gun	60	10,300
4.5in. howitzer	35	7,000
6in. howitzer	100	10,000–11,600
2.75in. mountain howitzer	12	5,800
3.7in. mountain howitzer	20	5,800

The Palestine Brigade Royal Air Force operated under Allenby's orders during the battle and was equipped with Bristol fighters, SE5As, DH9s, some Nieuports and a single Handley Page bomber capable of carrying sixteen 112lb bombs.

In terms of logistics, health and morale, Allenby's army was in excellent shape and was simply awaiting the opportunity to finish the war.

Across the Jordan, and working in concert with Allenby, was the Arab irregular army led by the Emir Feisal and Colonel T. E. Lawrence. This had the support of a British mechanised force which included a LAMB, a Light Car Patrol and a heavy section equipped with two Talbot lorries, each armed with a 10-pdr. mountain gun, and one Talbot mounting a Maxim pom-pom; a flight of aircraft; a company of the Egyptian Camel Corps and some logistic troops; and a small French detachment with two mountain guns and four machine guns, commanded by Captain Pisani. The small Arab regular army, commanded by Ja'far Pasha el Askeri, consisted of an infantry brigade, a camel battalion, a battalion of mule-mounted infantry and about eight guns. The irregular element of the army fluctuated wildly, depending upon success or failure and how close operations were to a tribe's home territory. All that can be said is that the army increased in proportion to the probability of Turkey's defeat. As to motivation, many of the Arabs nursed a profound hatred of the Turks, and the latter could expect little mercy if they fell into Arab hands.

These businesslike sowars of 18th King George's Own Lancers, photographed at Nazareth, reflect the professionalism of soldiering on the North West Frontier of India. Their lances lack pennons and their horses are hung about with water bottles and forage bags. Further points of interest are the spare bandoliers around the horses' necks and the tasselled fringes to keep flies off. (IWM Neg Q12350)

THE YILDERIM ARMY GROUP

As indicated earlier, the size of the Turkish army group in Palestine was largely governed by the number of troops that could be supported at the front. There had been no serious fighting in Palestine for several months and it might have been expected that the army group's deficiencies would have been made good during this time. This was not the case, for two reasons. First, Enver Pasha, the war minister, was allocating such resources as existed to the Caucasus Front, where Turkish troops had invaded the former Imperial Russian provinces with a view to securing the Baku oil fields for the Central Powers. Secondly, the Turkish war machine could not cope with the demands that were being made upon it, so everything, from uniforms and boots upwards, was in short supply.

Yilderim, in fact, was not an army group in the accepted sense since none of its composite armies was larger than a corps. It is true that the Ottoman Army as a whole had benefited from the German influence, but at the higher levels it remained a prey to indolent intrigue. The very name Yilderim, meaning 'lightning', was the subject of wry humour among attached German officers because of the leisurely manner in which affairs were conducted. There was, too, a serious cause of tension within the army. Arab officers and soldiers were treated as second class and had in the past been unfairly blamed for reverses; having been given a bad name and with little to lose, Arab conscripts had begun deserting before they reached a battlefield.

Liman von Sanders' cavalry were too few in number to present a serious challenge to the Desert Mounted Corps, but they could carry out reconnaissance and screening tasks efficiently and were certainly not lacking in spirit. The Anatolian element of the infantry consisted of hardy, stoical peasant soldiers who had shown themselves to be courageous, tough, vindictive fighters with a fondness for the bayonet. However, as they had never been required to display personal initiative,

Men of the Australian 5th Light Horse and the French 4th Chasseurs d'Afrique at Anebta on the second day of Megiddo. The French Arab and Barb mounts sometimes had trouble in keeping up with the big, hardy, Australian Walers. (IWM Neg Q12324)

their morale tended to collapse quickly if they were left leaderless and without orders. Unfortunately for them, by this stage of the war any close relationship that might have existed between them and their officers had largely disappeared and in consequence their welfare was neglected.

Thus, failure to apply the principles of hygiene in trench warfare conditions meant that an unacceptably high percentage of men were absent from the line at any one time, suffering from dysentery and other diseases. For all this, the expectations of the average Turkish soldier were lower than those of the soldiers confronting him in Palestine, and properly led, he would still fight stubbornly.

In sharp contrast, the German Asia Korps was, as might be expected, an adequately equipped, capably administered and well-led force, employed by Sanders to stiffen the Turkish armies. As the Order of Battle shows, it possessed considerable firepower and was the most formidable element in the Yilderim Army Group. Sanders' artillery – Turkish and Austro-German – was professionally handled and in the past its gunners had often fought to the muzzle. Its principal weapons were:

Type	Weight of shell (lb)	Range (yards)
75mm gun M'05	14	5,500
77mm gun (various models)	15	5,800/11,700
105mm howitzer (various models)	34	7,600/10,900
150mm howitzer (various models)	95	7,200/9,400

A very small number of Ehrhardt armoured cars were present but they were too slow and heavy to be of much use other than to provide a firebase for mobile operations; one at least was fitted with flanged wheels and used for railway patrol work.

The Yilderim Army Group was most vulnerable in the areas of logistics and internal command communications. It relied upon a ramshackle railway system backed by a small number of lorries and animal transport and depended heavily upon the telephone. If either of these systems were to be violently disrupted, the potential results would be very dangerous indeed; if both were to be disrupted simultaneously, as Allenby intended, the result could be little short of catastrophic.

The 12th Light Armoured Motor Battery and No. 7 Light Car Patrol on the road north of Aleppo. (IWM Neg Q12449)

ORDER OF BATTLE
EGYPTIAN EXPEDITIONARY FORCE
SEPTEMBER 1918

GENERAL HQ

Commander-in-Chief	General Sir Edmund Allenby, GCMG, KCB
Chief of General Staff	Major-general Sir L. J. Bols, KCMG, CB, DSO
Major General Royal Artillery	Major-general S. C. U. Smith, CB
Engineer-in-Chief	Major-general H. B. H. Wright, CB, CMG

DESERT MOUNTED CORPS

GOC Lieutenant-general Sir H. G. Chauvel, KCB, KCMG

CORPS TROOPS

Machine Gun Corps
Nos. 11 and 12 Light Armoured Motor Batteries
Nos. 1 and 7 Light Car Patrols

4TH CAVALRY DIVISION

GOC Major-general Sir G. de S. Barrow, KCMG, CB

10TH CAVALRY BRIGADE
Brigadier-general R. G. H. Howard-Vyse, CMG, DSO

I/1st Dorset Yeomanry
2nd Lancers
38th Central India Horse

11TH CAVALRY BRIGADE
Brigadier-general C. L. Gregory, CB

I/1st County of London (Middlesex) Yeomanry
29th Lancers
36th Jacob's Horse

12TH CAVALRY BRIGADE
Brigadier-general J. T. Wigan, DSO

I/1st Staffordshire Yeomanry
6th Cavalry
19th Lancers

ARTILLERY
XX Brigade RHA (Berks, Hants and Leicester Btys)

5TH CAVALRY DIVISION

GOC Major-general H. J. Macandrew, CB, DSO

13TH CAVALRY BRIGADE
Brigadier-general P. J. V. Kelly, CMG, DSO

I/1st Gloucestershire Yeomanry
9th Hodson's Horse
18th Lancers

14TH CAVALRY BRIGADE
Brigadier-general G. V. Clarke, DSO

I/1st Sherwood Rangers
20th Deccan Horse
34th Poona Horse

15TH (IMPERIAL SERVICE) CAVALRY BRIGADE
Brigadier-general C. R. Harboard, DSO

Jodhpore IS Lancers
Mysore IS Lancers
1st Hyderabad IS Lancers

ARTILLERY
Essex Battery RHA

AUSTRALIAN MOUNTED DIVISION

GOC Major-general H. W. Hodgson, CB, CVO

3RD AUSTRALIAN LIGHT HORSE BRIGADE
Brigadier-general L. C. Wilson, CMG

8th ALH
9th ALH
10th ALH

4TH AUSTRALIAN LIGHT HORSE BRIGADE
Brigadier-general W. Grant, DSO

4th ALH
11th ALH
12th ALH

5TH AUSTRALIAN LIGHT HORSE BRIGADE
Brigadier-general G. M. M. Onslow, DSO

14th ALH
15th ALH
Attached French Regiment Mixte Marche de Cavalerie

ARTILLERY
19 Brigade RHA (Notts Battery RHA, A & B Batteries HAC)

Tractor-hauled 60-pdr. gun. Flexibly handled heavy artillery achieved an overwhelming concentration of force on the sector chosen for the breakthrough. (IWM Neg Q24278)

XX CORPS

GOC Lieutenant-general Sir P. W. Chetwode, Bt, KCB, KCMG, DSO

CORPS TROOPS

MOUNTED
I/1st Worcestershire Yeomanry

ARTILLERY
97th Brigade Royal Garrison Artillery
103rd Brigade RGA
39th Indian Mountain Battery
Hong Kong & Singapore Mountain Battery

10TH DIVISION

GOC Major-general J. R. Longley, CB, CMG

29TH BRIGADE
Brigadier C. L. Smith, VC, MC

1st Leinster Regiment
I/54th Sikhs (FF)
I/101st Grenadiers
II/151st Indian Infantry

30TH BRIGADE
Brigadier-general F. A. Greer, CMG, DSO

1st Royal Irish Regiment
38th Dogras
1st Kashmir I S Infantry
46th Punjabis

31ST BRIGADE
Brigadier-general E. M. Morris, CMG

2nd Royal Irish Fusiliers

74th Punjabis
II/101st Grenadiers
II/42nd Deoli Regiment

ARTILLERY
67th Brigade RFA
68th Brigade RFA
263rd Brigade RFA

53RD DIVISION

GOC Major-general S. F. Mott, CB

158TH BRIGADE
Brigadier-general H. A. Vernon, DSO

V/6th Royal Welch Fusiliers
III/153rd Indian Infantry
IV/11th Gurkha Rifles
III/154th Indian Infantry

159TH BRIGADE
Brigadier-general N. E. Money, DSO

IV/5th Welch Regiment
I/153rd Indian Infantry
III/152nd Indian Infantry
II/153rd Indian Infantry

160TH BRIGADE
Brigadier-general V. L. N. Pearson

I/7th Royal Welch Fusiliers
I/21st Punjabis
I/17th Infantry
1st Cape Corps

ARTILLERY
265th Brigade RFA
266th Brigade RFA
267th Brigade RFA

Something – possibly the photographer – seems to have spooked the mules of the 2nd Bn. the Leicestershire Regiment's Lewis gun section and men are doubling forward to prevent them bolting in all directions. Taken on the coastal sector near Arsuf. (IWM Neg Q12508)

18-pdr. gun crew in action. (IWM Neg Q24267)

XXI CORPS

GOC Lieutenant-general Sir E. S. Bulfin, KCB, CVO

CORPS TROOPS

MOUNTED
Composite Regiment (one sqn. Duke of Lancaster's Yeomanry, two sqns. I/1st Hertfordshire Yeomanry)

ARTILLERY
95th Brigade RGA
96th Brigade RGA
100th Brigade RGA
102nd Brigade RGA
8th & 9th Mountain Brigades RGA

3RD INDIAN (LAHORE) DIVISION

GOC Major-general A. R. Hoskins, CMG, DSO

7TH BRIGADE
Brigadier-general S. R. Davidson, CMG

1st Connaught Rangers
II/7th Gurkha Rifles
27th Punjabis
91st Punjabis

8TH BRIGADE
Brigadier S. M. Edwardes, CB, CMG, DSO

1st Manchester Regiment
47th Sikhs
59th Scinde Rifles (FF)
II/124th Baluchistan Infantry

9TH BRIGADE
Brigadier-general C. C. Luard, CMG

2nd Dorsetshire Regiment
I/1st Gurkha Rifles
93rd Infantry
105th Mahratta Light Infantry

ARTILLERY
4th Brigade RFA
8th Brigade RFA
53rd Brigades RFA

7TH INDIAN (MEERUT) DIVISION

GOC Major-general Sir V. B. Fane, KCIE, CB

19TH BRIGADE
Brigadier-general G. A. Weir, DSO

1st Seaforth Highlanders
28th Punjabis
92nd Punjabis
125th Napier's Rifles

21ST BRIGADE
Brigadier-general A. G. Kemball

2nd Royal Highlanders
1st Guides Infantry
20th Punjabis
I/8th Gurkha Rifles

28TH BRIGADE (FF)
Brigadier-general C. H. Davies, CMG, DSO

2nd Leicestershire Regiment
51st Sikhs (FF)
53rd Sikhs (FF)
56th Punjabi Rifles (FF)

ARTILLERY
261st Brigade RFA
262nd Brigade RFA
264th Brigade RFA

54TH (EAST ANGLIAN) DIVISION

GOC Major-general S. W. Hare, CB

161ST BRIGADE
Brigadier-general H. B. H. Orpen-Palmer, DSO

I/4th Essex Regiment
I/5th Essex Regiment
I/6th Essex Regiment
I/7th Essex Regiment

162ND BRIGADE
Brigadier-general A. Mudge, CMG

I/5th Bedfordshire Regiment
I/4th Northamptonshire Regiment
I/10th London Regiment
I/11th London Regiment

163RD BRIGADE
Brigadier-general A. J. McNeill, DSO

I/4th Norfolk Regiment
I/5th Norfolk Regiment
I/5th Suffolk Regiment
I/8th Hampshire Regiment

ARTILLERY
270th Brigade RFA
271st Brigade RFA
272nd Brigade RFA

DÉTACHMENT FRANÇAIS DE PALESTINE ET SYRIE

(Under the orders of GOC 54th Division)
Commander Colonel P. de Péipape, CB

Régiment de Marche de Tirailleurs
7me Bn. 1er Tirailleurs Algériens
9me Bn. 2me Tirailleurs Algériens
Régiment de Marche de la Légion d'Orient
1er and 2me Bns Arméniens
One territorial battalion
One company Syrians
One squadron of dismounted Spahis

ARTILLERY
Three mountain batteries

60TH DIVISION

GOC Major-general J. S. M. Shea, CB, CMG, DSO

179TH BRIGADE
Brigadier-general E. T. Humphreys, DSO

II/13th London Regiment
III/151st Punjabi Rifles
II/19th Punjabis
II/127 Baluch Light Infantry

180TH BRIGADE
Brigadier-general C. F. Watson, CMG, DSO

II/19th London Regiment
2nd Guides Infantry
II/30th Punjabis
I/50th Kumaon Rifles

181ST BRIGADE
Brigadier-general E. C. Da Costa, CMG, DSO

II/22nd London Regiment
130th Baluchis
II/97th Deccan Infantry
II/152nd Indian Infantry

ARTILLERY
301st Brigade RFA
302nd Brigade RFA
303rd Brigade RFA

75TH DIVISION

GOC Major-general P. C. Palin, CB, CMG

232ND BRIGADE
Brigadier-general H. J. Huddleston, CMG, DSO, MC

I/4th Wiltshire Regiment
72nd Punjabis
II/3rd Gurkha Rifles
3rd Kashmir IS Infantry

233RD BRIGADE
Brigadier-general the Hon. E. M. Colston, CMG, DSO, MVO

I/5th Somerset Light Infantry
29th Punjabis
III/3rd Gurkha Rifles
II/154th Indian Infantry

234TH BRIGADE
Brigadier-general C. A. H. Maclean, DSO

I/4th Duke of Cornwall's Light Infantry
123rd Outram's Rifles
58th Vaughan's Rifles (FF)
I/152nd Indian Infantry

ARTILLERY
37th Brigade RFA
172nd Brigades RFA
1st South African FA Brigade

CHAYTOR'S FORCE

GOC Major-general Sir E. W. C. Chaytor, KCMG, CB (with staff of Australian and New Zealand Mounted Division)

AUSTRALIAN AND NEW ZEALAND MOUNTED DIVISION

1ST AUSTRALIAN LIGHT HORSE BRIGADE
Brigadier-general C. F. Fox, CB

1st ALH
2nd ALH
3rd ALH

2ND AUSTRALIAN LIGHT HORSE BRIGADE
Brigadier-general G. de L. Ryrie, CMG

5th ALH
6th ALH
7th ALH

NEW ZEALAND MOUNTED RIFLES BRIGADE
Brigadier-general W. Meldrum, CB, DSO

Auckland MR
Canterbury MR
Wellington MR

20TH INDIAN BRIGADE
Brigadier-general E. R. B. Murray

Alwar IS Infantry
Gwalior IS Infantry
Patiala IS Infantry
110th Mahratta Light Infantry

INDEPENDENT INFANTRY BATTALIONS
38th Royal Fusiliers
39th Royal Fusiliers
1st West Indies Regiment
2nd West Indies Regiment

ARTILLERY
18th Brigade RHA (Inverness, Ayr & Somerset Batteries)
75th Battery RFA
29th & 32nd Indian Mountain Batteries
195th Heavy Battery RGA

ROYAL AIR FORCE MIDDLE EAST

GOC Major-general W. G. H. Salmond, DSO

PALESTINE BRIGADE RAF

Brigadier-general A. E. Borton, DSO

5TH (CORPS) WING
14 Sqn.
113 Sqn.
142 Sqn.

40TH (ARMY) WING
111 Sqn.
144 Sqn.
145 Sqn.
1 Sqn Australian FC
No 21 Balloon Company

Total	Cavalry:	11,000
	Infantry:	56,000
	Guns:	552

Notes on the above

FF Frontier Force, one of the Indian army's elite formations, regularly engaged on the North West Frontier

IS Imperial Service, units provided by the rulers of Indian princely states for service with the Crown

RHA Royal Horse Artillery, serving with mounted formations

RFA Royal Field Artillery, serving with infantry formations

RGA Royal Garrison Artillery, heavy artillery units usually serving as corps troops

The armament of horse artillery batteries was usually four 13-pdr. (sometimes 18-pdr.) guns; field batteries had six 18-pdr. guns, save for the third battery of a field artillery brigade, which was equipped with four 4.5in. howitzers. Mountain batteries were armed with 3.7in. howitzers or 2.75in. guns. Heavy artillery weapons included the 8in. howitzer, the 6in. gun, 60-pdr. and 6in. howitzers. Where adequate supplies of ammunition existed and sufficient personnel were available, captured 150mm and 105mm howitzers and 75mm guns were also incorporated in the fire plan.

Each mounted brigade had a machine gun squadron and each infantry brigade a machine gun company and a light trench mortar battery.

ORDER OF BATTLE
YILDERIM ARMY GROUP
SEPTEMBER 1918

Commander-in-Chief
   General Liman von Sanders
Chief of Staff   General Kiazim Pasha

GENERAL HQ TROOPS
   109th Regiment (attached to Seventh Army)
   110th Regiment
   13th Depot Regiment
   17th Depot Regiment

YILDERIM FLYING COMMAND
   1st Pursuit Detachment
   302nd Reconnaissance Detachment
   303rd Reconnaissance Detachment
   304th Reconnaissance Detachment

FOURTH ARMY
GOC   General Mohammed Djemal Kuçuk

ARMY TROOPS

3RD CAVALRY DIVISION

   63rd Infantry Regiment
   German 146th Infantry Regiment

II CORPS

HAURAN DETACHMENT
AMMAN DIVISION
MA'AN DETACHMENT

VIII CORPS

Colonel Ali Fuad Bey

CAUCASUS CAVALRY BRIGADE

48TH DIVISION
COMPOSITE DIVISION
   Mule-mounted Infantry Regiment
   Independent Infantry Battalions etc, east of
   the Jordan

Djemal Kuçuk confers with his Chief of Staff at Field Headquarters Turkish Fourth Army during an exercise. Other figures of interest are the Naval ADC and the Circassian bodyguard sporting a long kinjal dagger. (Dr David Nicolle)

SEVENTH ARMY

GOC General Mustapha Kemal Pasha

III CORPS

Colonel Ismet Bey

1ST DIVISION
11TH DIVISION

XX CORPS

Major-general Ali Fuad Pasha

24TH DIVISION
26TH DIVISION
53RD DIVISION

EIGHTH ARMY

GOC General Djevad Pasha

ARMY TROOPS

46TH DIVISION

XXII CORPS

Colonel Refet Bey

7TH DIVISION
20TH DIVISION

Turkish cavalry passing through Beersheba in review order, April 1917. Though brave enough, the Turkish cavalry was neither suffiently well mounted nor numerous enough to seriously challenge the Desert Mounted Corps. (Dr David Nicolle)

ASIA KORPS

Colonel von Oppen

16TH DIVISION
19TH DIVISION

GERMAN PASHA II BRIGADE
- 701st Infantry Battalion
- 702nd Infantry Battalion
- 703rd Infantry Battalion
- 701st Artillery Detachment (two 4-gun 77mm batteries and one 4-gun 105mm howitzer battery)
- Machine Gun Detachment 'Hentig'

PASHA II REINFORCEMENTS
(Lieutenant Colonel Freiherr von Hammerstein-Gesmold)

- Masurian Infantry Regiment 146 (three battalions each with six machine guns)
- 11th Reserve Jäger Battalion (with six machine guns)
- Mountain Artillery Detachment (three 4-gun howitzer batteries)
- Mountain Machine Gun Detachment (four machine gun companies)

Total
- Cavalry: 3,000
- Infantry: 32,000
- Guns: 370

Turkish and German Fourth Army Staff officers, some in summer uniform, pose for the camera shortly before Megiddo. The Fourth Army survived the initial onslaught but its remnants were destroyed at Damascus. (IWM Neg Q82517)

Notes on the above
The German 701st, 702nd and 703rd battalions each possessed six machine guns and 18 Bergman light machine guns. In addition, to each battalion was attached a machine gun company of six guns, a troop of cavalry, an assault gun platoon with two mountain guns or howitzers, and a trench mortar section with four mortars. It can thus be seen that while in terms of infantry the German presence amounted to only seven battalions, it possessed the firepower of a division in local circumstances.

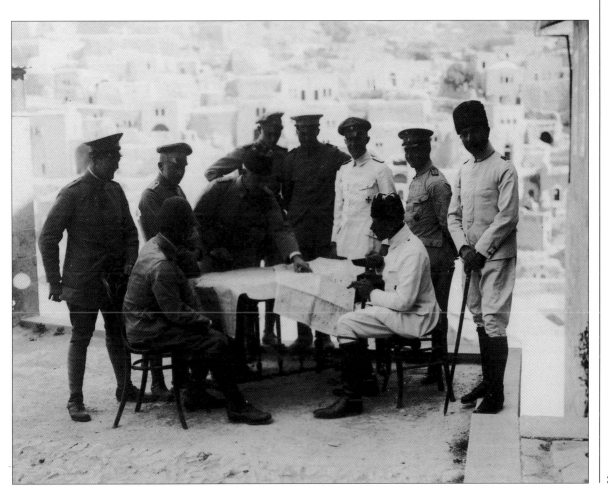

OPPOSING PLANS

ALLENBY'S PLAN

Three major factors influenced Allenby's planning for the Battle of Megiddo. The first was that neither the number of the enemy's guns and machine guns per mile of front, nor the width of his wire, nor the overall depth of his defences came close to approaching that of the Western Front and this in itself enhanced the possibility of achieving a clean breakthrough on a narrow sector. The second was that much of the enemy hinterland consisted of good cavalry country in which the Desert Mounted Corps could be used to best effect. The third was the dispositions of the Turks. General von Falkenhayn, Sanders' predecessor, had intended to execute a voluntary strategic withdrawal to the more easily defended watercourse of the Nahr Iskenderun, which ran through Tul Karm to the sea. Sanders, however, preoccupied as he was with the concept of holding ground for its own sake, had refused to sanction this, with the result that his right flank still rested on the sea in a not especially favourable position, some ten miles north of Jaffa.

Allenby's intention was to destroy Sanders' army group at a stroke. An infantry breakthrough on the coastal sector would be exploited with a huge wheel to the right by the Desert Mounted Corps, thus severing Turkish communications as it carved its way to the Jordan valley. In

German-trained Turkish storm-troopers being inspected by a senior officer, Palestine, summer 1918. They are wearing a local variant of the German steel helmet. Unfortunately for them, the battle they would fight was very different from that for which they had been trained. (Dr David Nicolle)

Turkish machine gun school. The position of each detachment member, observer and the water-cooled weapon's condenser unit are clearly shown. In this category of weapon the Turkish division was actually better equipped than the British infantry division. (Dr David Nicolle)

essence the plan was very simple; the genius lay in its attention to detail.

The breakthrough would be made by Lieutenant-general Sir Edward Bulfin's XXI Corps, deployed with, from the right, the 54th, 3rd Indian, 75th, 7th Indian and 60th divisions, along a 15-mile sector of front close to the coast. Logically, therefore, the bulk of Allenby's artillery was allocated to XXI Corps, under the direction of Brigadier-general H. A. D. Simpson-Baikie, the Corps' brigadier Royal Artillery. Altogether there would be five 60-pdr. and 13 siege batteries, the artillery of the five infantry divisions and the French Detachment, plus two mountain batteries. Seven RHA batteries of the Desert Mounted Corps would take part in the early phases of the bombardment and then return to their own divisions, and some immobile 4.7in. guns and captured weapons would complete a grand total of 258 guns and 126 howitzers, three-quarters of which would be deployed on the seven-mile sector closest to the sea. Off the coast, the destroyers HMS *Druid* and *Forester* would provide direct gunfire support on the enemy's trenches. Just behind and overlaying the rear areas of XXI Corps would be Lieutenant-general Sir Harry Chauvel's Desert Mounted Corps, ready to exploit the breakthrough.

Along the remaining 45 miles of front Allenby had only Lieutenant-general Sir P. W. Chetwode's XX Corps (53rd and 10th divisions) and Major-general Sir E. W. C. Chaytor's force (the ANZAC Mounted Division and two infantry brigades). XX Corps possessed one 60-pdr. and four siege howitzer batteries, two mountain batteries and seven captured guns. With the divisional artillery this made a total of 86 guns and 44 howitzers; Chaytor's force had four 60-pdr. guns, four 18-pdrs., twelve 2.75in. mountain guns, four captured 75mm guns, two captured 150mm howitzers and the twelve 13-pdr. guns of the ANZAC Mounted Division.

Every aspect of Allenby's offensive had received the closest scrutiny. The artillery, for example, had established means of getting some of its heavy guns forward once the front had been broken. The engineers had assembled equipment, including trestle and pontoon bridges, which would enable cavalry, guns and wheeled transport to cross the captured trench lines and other obstacles without delay. Major-general M. G. E. Bowman-Manifold, director of army signals, had taken great pains to ensure that communications were maintained between the advancing spearheads and the higher headquarters. Whenever possible, Turkish overhead telephone cables, all of which were carefully marked, were to be taken into service to save time and British wire, and divisions were instructed to set up radio stations whenever possible. In appropriate circumstances it was also planned to use heliograph, carrier pigeons and despatch riders, who would be motorcyclists by day and cavalrymen by night or in difficult country.

Although the railhead from Egypt had reached Lod, supply problems still existed. For example, each cavalry, artillery and transport horse consumed an average 20lb feed per day, and since animal transport would be too slow to meet divisional requirements for long, a fleet of lorries had been built up to cope with this – 240 had been allocated to XXI Corps, 180 to XX Corps, 150 to the Desert Mounted Corps and 20 to Chaytor's force.

Water was not the acute problem it had been once, but as Bulfin's infantry divisions would be advancing into difficult country, XXI Corps was allocated two camel transport corps water columns, each consisting of two companies with 2,200 camels carrying a total of 44,000 gallons. To allow for unexpected contingencies, a number of pumping engines were to be carried. On the day of the attack the troops would be issued with that day's ration, two days' emergency rations and iron rations.

The Royal Air Force was to play a vital role in Allenby's plan. First, at the strategic level, it would destroy Sanders' telephone links and so paralyse

Turkish field gunners engaging a target with indirect fire. The signaller, left, is repeating the forward observation officer's corrections, which are being plotted on the artillery board in the gunpit. (Dr David Nicolle)

Turkish signal detachment at work. Their equipment includes a signal lamp/heliograph, a theodolite for checking bearings and a telescope for reading the reply, which is being duly logged. After the Yilderim telephone and radio network had been eliminated, this was often the only means of communication. (Dr David Nicolle)

command of his army group. Then, tactically, it would, by continuous strafing of Turkish columns retreating from the front, break the enemy's will to continue the fight. In the meantime, its task was to prevent Turkish and German airmen discovering the preparations for the forthcoming offensive by keeping them out of Allied air space. In this it succeeded so well that only four enemy machines were able to cross the lines in the week before the offensive began.

Equally vital was Allenby's deception plan, which was designed to convince Sanders that he intended attacking in the Jordan valley instead of on the coastal sector. Working in harsh, hot conditions, Chaytor's force played the major role in this, constructing dummy camps from old, worn tents, dummy gun parks and battery positions built from old wheels, pipes and logs, and dummy horses made from wood frames, blankets and canvas, assembled into formal horse lines to suggest that the entire Desert Mounted Corps was present. The whole was accompanied by continuous bustle, mule-drawn sledges raising huge dust clouds, and the lighting of many campfires. Simultaneously the Arab army intensified its efforts against the Hejaz railway, particularly against the important junction at Deraa. At the other end of the line the situation was reversed. Troops assembling for the attack moved by night into concealed bivouacs among the orange groves or into camps the size of which had been increased two months earlier. They remained under cover during the hours of daylight and were permitted no fires at any time – cooking was done with smokeless solidified alcohol.

From the Turkish side of the lines, therefore, there was nothing to suggest that any abnormal activity was taking place. Secrecy was of such importance that objectives were only given to brigade and regimental commanders two or three days before the attack. Allenby then visited each division in turn and explained his plan to the assembled commanding officers. Its sheer scope and his unbounded confidence that it would be fulfilled made an unforgettable impression on his audience. Meanwhile, two pieces of information had been leaked to the civil population in the certain knowledge that Turkish sympathisers would carry them straight to Sanders. The first was that the General Headquarters was about to move into the best hotel in Jerusalem, and the second was that there would be an important race meeting near Jaffa on 19 September.

SANDERS' PLAN

On 19 September 1918 Sanders had three armies immediately available for the coming battle. On the right Djevad Pasha's Eighth Army of 10,000 men and 157 guns included most of the Asia Korps and held a 20-mile front from the sea to Furqa. From Furqa to the Jordan valley the front became the responsibility of Mustapha Kemal's Seventh Army, with a strength of 7,000 men and 111 guns. The Trans-Jordan and desert flank was held by Djemal Kuçuk's Fourth Army with 8,000 men and 74 guns. In army group reserve were 3,000 men and 30 guns, including the German 146th Regiment. Further afield, some 6,000 men were deployed along the Hejaz railway, but of these only the garrison of Amman was likely to become involved in the battle. To the north, and spread across a wide area between Damascus and the Taurus, was the Second Army, with some 5,000 men – too weak and too distant to offer decisive intervention.

These figures are based on British intelligence estimates and, as Cyril Falls, the author of the Official History, points out, may err a little on the low side. Turkish quartermasters were in the habit of inflating a formation's 'ration strength' to two or three times its 'rifle strength' for their own personal gain. The fraud, however, was not quite so blatant as it appears, as 'rifle strength' simply meant riflemen and did not include machine gunners, of whom there were 800 in each division.

The Turkish division, however weak in numbers, possessed 60 heavy machine guns – more than the British division. Including the Asia Korps,

An Asia Korps detachment, with band, showing the flag in a Palestinian town. (Bundesarchiv Neg 77/101/36)

Asia Korps stretcher bearers and camel with casualty evacuation litters; they are wearing a peaked version of the German 'pork pie' forage cap. (Bundesarchiv Neg 71/103/36)

Sanders deployed 600 heavy machine guns west of the Jordan against 350 British and French. In light machine guns the Allies had the advantage, but there were still about 450 of these weapons in Turkish and German units west of the river.

On balance, therefore, Allenby enjoyed a numerical superiority of about two to one, but as the accepted ratio for a successful attack on an enemy has always been set at three to one, Sanders felt reasonably secure. His dispositions were made solely with static defence in mind, and no contingency plan existed for a large-scale withdrawal.

However, Sanders had two Achilles' heels. The first lay in the siting of his General Headquarters too far behind the front, at Nazareth, connected to Eighth Army HQ at Tul Karm, Seventh Army HQ at Nablus and Fourth Army HQ at Es Salt by a telephone line that ran through a single main switchboard at Afula. He had fallen completely for Allenby's deception plan, and until the offensive opened, Sanders believed that the Desert Mounted Corps was in the Jordan valley. Thus, most of the

The Handley Page 0/400 heavy bomber carried a 1,650lb bombload and had a maximum speed of 97mph. The one such aircraft available to the RAF in Palestine was known to the Arabs as The Aeroplane, all other aircraft being its children. (IWM Neg Q68141)

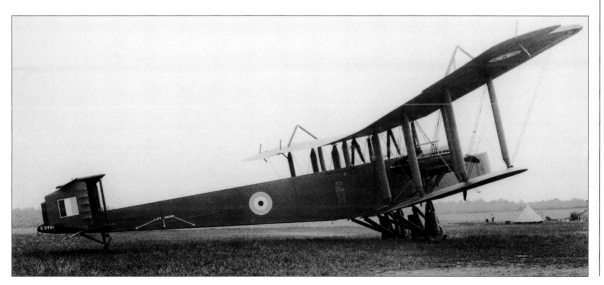

Turkish strength (the 15,000 men and 185 guns of the Fourth and Seventh armies) was deployed to meet an attack on that sector.

As luck would have it, a havildar of the 7th Indian Division was captured on 17 September and is believed to have revealed much of the real plan. Djevad and the commander of the Turkish XXII Corps, upon whom the weight of the blow would fall, were sufficiently convinced to request permission for a tactical withdrawal so that the Allied bombardment would land on empty trenches, but Sanders thought that the prisoner was a plant and refused. Thus, when the moment came on the critical coastal sector, 8,000 Turks with 130 guns suddenly found themselves against a force of 35,000 infantry and 9,000 cavalry with 383 guns. Allenby had achieved the odds he sought and his battle was won before the first shot had been fired.

AMMUNITION SCALE ALLIED ARMY 19 SEPTEMBER 1918

Mobile Guns	Rounds Each
13-pdr.	1,100
18-pdr.	1,000
2.75in. gun	1,000
3.7in. gun	800
4.5in. howitzer	800
6in. howitzer	800
60-pdr. gun	800

Of this, 450 rounds per gun were to be carried by units. For immediate replenishment the corps had 150 rounds ready loaded in their lorries and another 500 dumped at suitable points.

Immobile Guns	Rounds Each
8in. howitzer	400
6in. Mk VII	250
60-pdr. gun & 6in. howitzer	500
French	700
150mm captured	250
105mm captured	250
75mm & 77mm captured	400
Anti-aircraft	600

ALLIED TRANSPORT

Formation	Donkey Coys.	Camel Coys.	Tractors	Trucks	Lorries Ammn.	Lorries Supply
Chaytor's Force	300 Donkeys	–	17	34	5	14
DMC	–	2	–	–	30	120
XX Corps	2	1	–	–	60	120
XXI Corps	1	8	12	24	60	180
Total	3 + 300 Donkeys	11	29	58	155	435

THE BATTLE OF MEGIDDO

19 September

During the night of 18–19 September Chetwode's XX Corps mounted a heavy diversionary attack intended to reinforce Sanders' suspicions that Allenby was about to launch an offensive up the Jordan valley. Shortly after midnight the RAF became active, bombing the headquarters of the Turkish Seventh and Eighth armies, while the single Handley Page bomber raided Afula, wrecking the main telephone exchange. As a result of these air attacks, the telephone communications of all three Turkish armies and the Eighth Army's radio stations were put out of action, ensuring that Sanders would begin the battle without effective command of his troops.

However, for those Turks positioned on the centre and right of Sanders' line, the night seemed like any other. Both sides sent out patrols as usual, and there were brief clashes in No Man's Land, but nothing occurred to suggest anything untoward was about to happen.

Taking advantage of the period of darkness between moonset and first light, the infantrymen of Bulfin's XXI Corps were silently leaving their trenches and moving forward to previously taped start lines at right angles to their axes of advance. Then, at 04:30, the British bombardment suddenly thundered out. It was the heaviest ever mounted in this theatre of war and at its height over 1,000 shells per minute were exploding in the enemy's lines, from which alarm rockets began streaking skyward. The Turkish artillery responded at once, but most of its counter-bombardment

The RAF not only destroyed the enemy's communications but also kept Turkish and German aircraft grounded by constant patrolling above their airfields. Seen here are two wrecked aircraft on Jenin airfield, captured by 3rd Light Horse Brigade on 20 September. (IWM Neg Q12344)

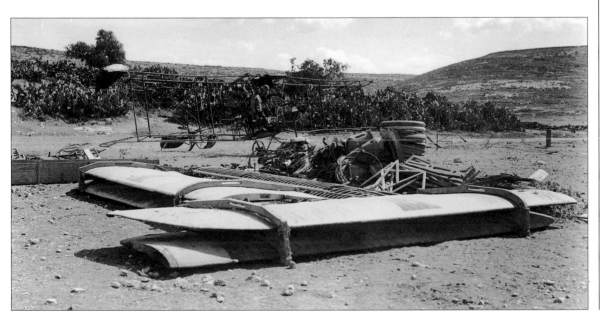

landed in the recently vacated trenches. Even the fire of those batteries that had been adjusted to engage the British infantry, now rapidly advancing across the 1,000 yards of No Man's Land, was quickly suppressed by the heavy artillery's counter-battery fire. Where Turkish fire persisted, it soon became ragged, so that platoon commanders found no difficulty in leading their men through obvious gaps in the defensive barrage.

Bulfin's infantry came on very quickly. Here and there a man fell, but the impetus of the attack could not be halted. On reaching the Turkish lines, now smothered under a pall of dust and smoke, the thin belt of wire was soon breached with planks, corrugated iron or stuffed sandbags. A flurry of grenades exploded around the parapets and then the attackers went in with the bayonet. Most of the Turks were too stunned or confused by events to offer resistance and there were mass surrenders. Behind a carefully controlled creeping barrage, successive waves took up the advance to secure the second and reserve line of trenches, suddenly finding themselves in open country with crowds of distant Turkish fugitives streaming away to the north and north-east.

Everywhere there were signs that the hammer blow had shattered the enemy's will to fight. On the 7th (Meerut) Division's sector alone, numerous examples were quoted of his complete collapse. A 150mm howitzer battery was captured by a wounded NCO, Naik (Lance Corporal) Buta Khan of the 92nd Punjabis, and four wounded men of the 1st Guides; 40 men of the 125th Rifles took 200 prisoners and six machine guns; and Captain T. W. Rees and six men of the same battalion took a battery of three 105mm howitzers.

In effect, the Turkish XXII Corps, closest to the coast, had been destroyed at a stroke. Its commander, Refet Bey, became a fugitive behind British lines for the better part of a week, but eventually managed to reach Tyre just before it was occupied.

The 3rd (Lahore), 7th (Meerut) and 60th Division now began swinging eastwards like an opening door to create a protective hard shoulder for the gap through which the Desert Mounted Corps was streaming. Major-general J. S. M. Shea's 60th Division, with Brigadier G. M. M.

HMS *Forester*, one of two I (Acheron) Class destroyers that provided direct naval gunfire support on the first day of Megiddo. To have employed larger warships would have raised Turkish suspicions. Armament consisted of two 4in. and two 12-pdr. guns. (IWM Neg SP924)

Onslow's 5th Light Horse Brigade under command, had furthest to go, but Shea was an experienced commander and pushed his men hard. His objective was Tul Karm, which until a few hours earlier had housed the HQ of the Turkish Eighth Army.

THE SITUATION AT ZERO HOUR, 19 SEPTEMBER 1918

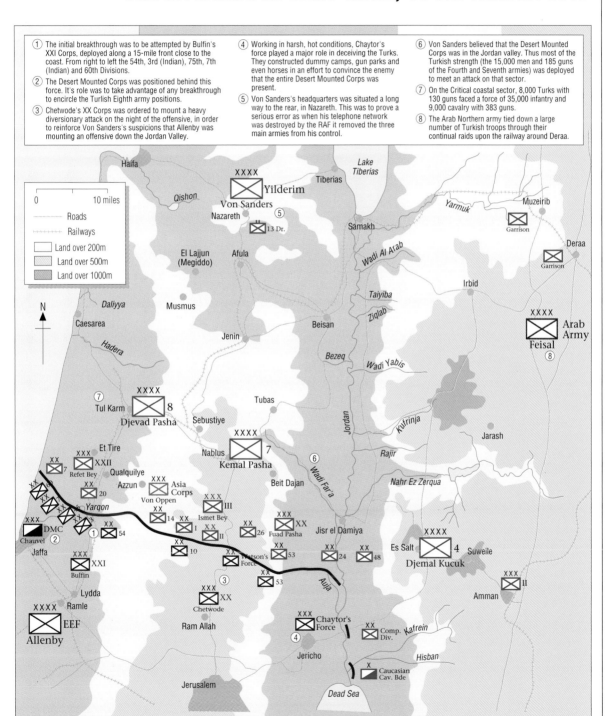

① The initial breakthrough was to be attempted by Bulfin's XXI Corps, deployed along a 15-mile front close to the coast. From right to left the 54th, 3rd (Indian), 75th, 7th (Indian) and 60th Divisions.

② The Desert Mounted Corps was positioned behind this force. It's role was to take advantage of any breakthrough to encircle the Turlish Eighth army positions.

③ Chetwode's XX Corps was ordered to mount a heavy diversionary attack on the night of the offensive, in order to reinforce Von Sanders's suspicions that Allenby was mounting an offensive down the Jordan Valley.

④ Working in harsh, hot conditions, Chaytor's force played a major role in deceiving the Turks. They constructed dummy camps, gun parks and even horses in an effort to convince the enemy that the entire Desert Mounted Corps was present.

⑤ Von Sanders's headquarters was situated a long way to the rear, in Nazareth. This was to prove a serious error as when his telephone network was destroyed by the RAF it removed the three main armies from his control.

⑥ Von Sanders believed that the Desert Mounted Corps was in the Jordan valley. Thus most of the Turkish strength (the 15,000 men and 185 guns of the Fourth and Seventh armies) was deployed to meet an attack on that sector.

⑦ On the Critical coastal sector, 8,000 Turks with 130 guns faced a force of 35,000 infantry and 9,000 cavalry with 383 guns.

⑧ The Arab Northern army tied down a large number of Turkish troops through their continual raids upon the railway around Deraa.

The original plan required Onslow to capture Tul Karm and hand it over when the main body of 60th Division arrived, but Shea had modified this slightly, telling him to disregard the town if he ran into serious resistance and concentrate instead on cutting the road eastwards to Nablus. The brigade passed through 7th Division and by noon had reached a point west of the town. Here one squadron of the 15th Light Horse was detached in pursuit of an enemy column retreating from Irta while the rest of the brigade moved off into the foothills north and north-east of Tul Karm. A spirited charge by a squadron of the French Régiment Mixte resulted in the capture of an Austrian battery position 2,000 yards north of the town. Having circled Tul Karm, the defences of which clearly incorporated numerous machine guns, Onslow decided to exercise his option and pursue the swarms of fugitives fleeing along the road to Nablus. These were simultaneously bombed and machine gunned from the air, engaged with dismounted fire from the hillsides or ridden down in local charges.

Such was the degree of panic afflicting the Turks that overturned vehicles blocked the road at several points and they willingly surrendered in large numbers. Altogether, the brigade took some 2,000 prisoners, 15 guns and a large haul of supplies. One enemy column did manage to break free of the road and head north through Shuweike, but the French were sent in pursuit and returned next morning with several hundred more prisoners. At 17:00 the 60th Division, having conducted a fighting advance of sixteen and a half miles in twelve and a half hours, captured Tul Karm, the garrison of which, now knowing itself to be cut off, had been further demoralised by air attack. A further 500 Turks marched into captivity and a dozen more guns were taken.

Meanwhile, near the coast, the Desert Mounted Corps was pouring through the gap that had been opened by XXI Corps' infantry. In the lead were the 4th Cavalry Division on the right and 5th Cavalry Division on the left. Their commanders had spent the previous night at the

Heavy howitzer in action. On the coastal sector the bombardment left the defenders stunned and smothered any attempt at counter-battery fire. (IWM Neg Q24240)

A 1,200-strong column of prisoners, taken by the Desert Mounted Corps, marches into captivity along the Kerkur–Tul Karm road, escorted by men of 181st Brigade, 60th Division. (IWM Neg Q12326)

headquarters of the infantry divisions that were to create the gap so that their troops could be set in motion at the earliest possible moment. The move of the two divisions into their assembly areas, obstacle clearing, route marking, trench ramping and the return of the RHA batteries after their part in the initial bombardment had all gone according to plan and both, followed by the Australian Mounted Division, had begun moving at a cracking pace over the good cavalry country of the Plain of Sharon. On the coast itself naval gunfire support eased the passage of Major-general Macandrew's 5th Cavalry Division, and elsewhere the enemy's resistance was negligible; one trooper of the Gloucester Hussars personally captured two guns, an officer and 20 men, and another captured 37 wagons, four officers and 100 men.

A torrent of horsemen was now sweeping north so quickly that the Turks, even if their communications had been intact, would have been unable to react. The task of the 4th Cavalry Division, with the 11th LAMB and 1st LCP attached, was to secure the Musmus Pass and cut the railway near Afula. A detachment was then to be sent to seize the bridges over the Jordan and Yarmuk at Jisr el Majami while the main body advanced on Beisan. The 5th Cavalry Division, with 12th LAMB and 7th LCP attached, was to continue northwards to Abu Shushe, where it was to send a detachment to Nazareth with the object of capturing Sanders' GHQ and, if possible, Sanders himself, and be prepared to 'operate towards Jenin and Beisan according to circumstances'. The Australian Mounted Division, less the 5th Light Horse Brigade, was to follow the 4th Cavalry Division as corps reserve and be prepared to detach a brigade from El Lajjun to block the Damascus road and railway at Jenin.

The enemy, when encountered, usually fled or surrendered at once, although there were isolated pockets of resistance, such as that at Nahr Falik. There some 200 Turks and two guns were overrun by D Squadron 9th Hodson's Horse: the guns and 50 men were captured at a cost of one killed and two wounded. On the other hand, the corps' horses had

INITIAL BREAKTHROUGH

The Situation at 12 midnight on 19–20 September 1918.

Von Sanders directed Major Frey, Inspector General of Pioneers, to occupy the mouth of the Musmus Pass at El Lajjun, putting at his disposal the best of the 13th Depot Regiment at Nazareth and all the military police on whom he could lay his hands – a total of six companies and 12 machine guns.

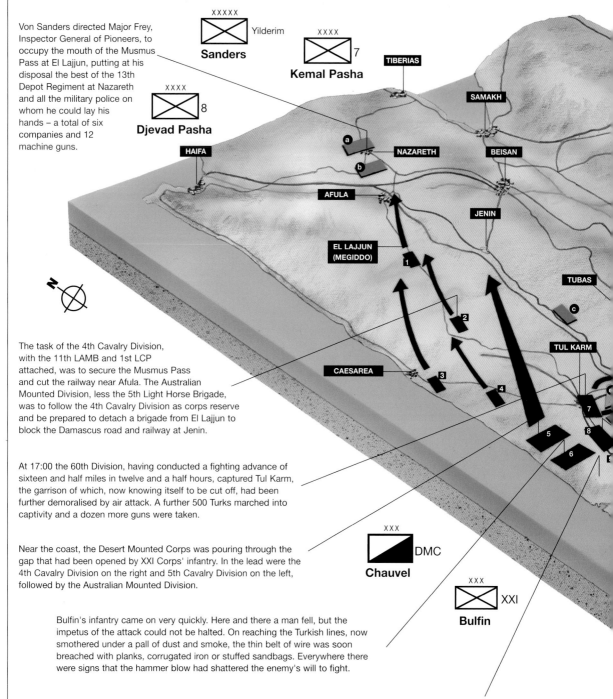

The task of the 4th Cavalry Division, with the 11th LAMB and 1st LCP attached, was to secure the Musmus Pass and cut the railway near Afula. The Australian Mounted Division, less the 5th Light Horse Brigade, was to follow the 4th Cavalry Division as corps reserve and be prepared to detach a brigade from El Lajjun to block the Damascus road and railway at Jenin.

At 17:00 the 60th Division, having conducted a fighting advance of sixteen and half miles in twelve and a half hours, captured Tul Karm, the garrison of which, now knowing itself to be cut off, had been further demoralised by air attack. A further 500 Turks marched into captivity and a dozen more guns were taken.

Near the coast, the Desert Mounted Corps was pouring through the gap that had been opened by XXI Corps' infantry. In the lead were the 4th Cavalry Division on the right and 5th Cavalry Division on the left, followed by the Australian Mounted Division.

Bulfin's infantry came on very quickly. Here and there a man fell, but the impetus of the attack could not be halted. On reaching the Turkish lines, now smothered under a pall of dust and smoke, the thin belt of wire was soon breached with planks, corrugated iron or stuffed sandbags. Everywhere there were signs that the hammer blow had shattered the enemy's will to fight.

Taking advantage of the period of darkness between moonset and first light, the infantrymen of Bulfin's XXI Corps were silently leaving their trenches and moving forward to previously taped start lines at right angles to their axes of advance. Then, at 04:30, the British bombardment suddenly thundered out. It was the heaviest ever mounted in this theatre of war and at its height over 1,000 shells per minute were exploding in the enemy's lines, from which alarm rockets began streaking skyward.

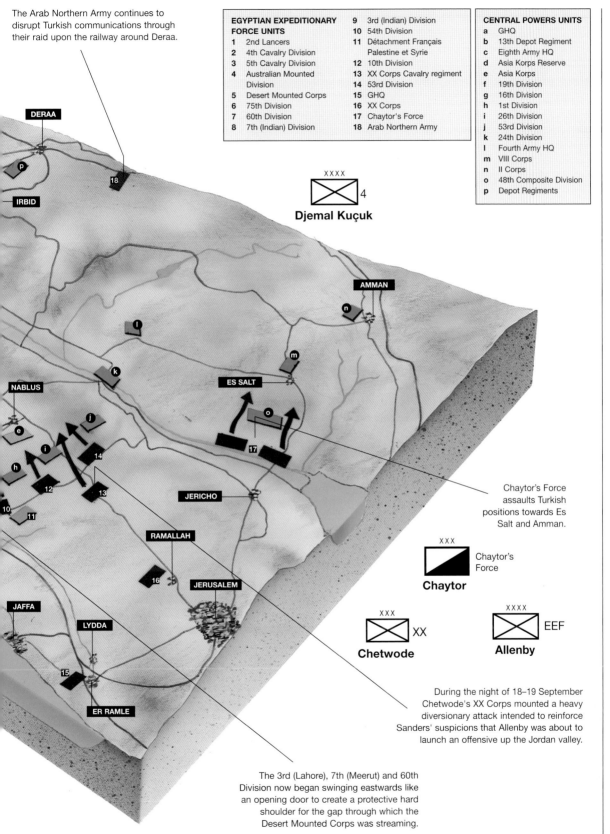

The Arab Northern Army continues to disrupt Turkish communications through their raid upon the railway around Deraa.

EGYPTIAN EXPEDITIONARY FORCE UNITS

1	2nd Lancers
2	4th Cavalry Division
3	5th Cavalry Division
4	Australian Mounted Division
5	Desert Mounted Corps
6	75th Division
7	60th Division
8	7th (Indian) Division
9	3rd (Indian) Division
10	54th Division
11	Détachment Français Palestine et Syrie
12	10th Division
13	XX Corps Cavalry regiment
14	53rd Division
15	GHQ
16	XX Corps
17	Chaytor's Force
18	Arab Northern Army

CENTRAL POWERS UNITS

a	GHQ
b	13th Depot Regiment
c	Eighth Army HQ
d	Asia Korps Reserve
e	Asia Korps
f	19th Division
g	16th Division
h	1st Division
i	26th Division
j	53rd Division
k	24th Division
l	Fourth Army HQ
m	VIII Corps
n	II Corps
o	48th Composite Division
p	Depot Regiments

XXXX
4
Djemal Kuçuk

Chaytor's Force assaults Turkish positions towards Es Salt and Amman.

XXX
Chaytor's Force
Chaytor

XXX
XX
Chetwode

XXXX
EEF
Allenby

During the night of 18–19 September Chetwode's XX Corps mounted a heavy diversionary attack intended to reinforce Sanders' suspicions that Allenby was about to launch an offensive up the Jordan valley.

The 3rd (Lahore), 7th (Meerut) and 60th Division now began swinging eastwards like an opening door to create a protective hard shoulder for the gap through which the Desert Mounted Corps was streaming.

43

suffered severely from the forced pace and a number, having foundered, had to be destroyed.

During the evening a halt was made for watering and rest, since the commanders of both cavalry divisions recognised that if the enemy was going to make a stand he would do so in the Samarian Hills, which separated them from the Plain of Esdraelon. Movement would therefore continue overnight and the next few hours would be critical.

Throughout 19 September Liman von Sanders was left groping in a fog of war. All communication with HQ Eighth Army at Tul Karm had ceased at 07:00, but two hours later he received a message from Colonel von Oppen, routed through HQ Seventh Army, to the effect that the coastal sector had been pierced and that British cavalry was advancing northwards. Oppen, it seemed, was constructing a defensive front between Nablus and Tul Karm, and Seventh Army, while apparently holding, was pulling back to its second line.

Further communications were disrupted by more air attacks on the main switchboard at Afula. Again, as the RAF had effectively grounded Sanders' air force by sitting above its airfields, he had no idea what was taking place on the ground. He believed, for example, that the Turkish XXII Corps was retiring before the British advance when, of course, it had ceased to exist. Nevertheless, by 12:30 he had made some allowance for the worst that might happen and directed Major Frey, Inspector General of Pioneers, to occupy the mouth of the Musmus Pass at El Lajjun, putting at his disposal the best of the 13th Depot Regiment at Nazareth and all the military police on whom he could lay his hands – a total of six companies and 12 machine guns. Why he specified the mouth rather than the more easily defended summit of the pass remains a mystery.

20 September

The pattern of fighting during the second day of the battle saw XX and XXI Corps maintaining pressure on the Turkish Seventh and Eighth armies, which continued to give ground, despite the stiff resistance offered by the German Asia Korps. Djevad Pasha briefly re-established his Eighth Army HQ at Masudiye Station, striving vainly to impose some sort of order on his fleeing troops. To the north, the Desert Mounted Corps wheeled north-eastwards across the Turkish rear, with dramatic results.

A captured 5.9in. howitzer, limber and towing vehicle taken into British service on the Nablus–Beisan road. (IWM Neg Q12312)

Divisional transport crossing a pontoon bridge spanning the River Auja. An integral part of Allenby's planning was the rapid follow-up of logistic elements in the wake of the breakthrough. (IWM Neg Q12971)

Major-general Macandrew's 5th Cavalry Division advanced on a one brigade frontage throughout the night, led by Brigadier-general P. J. V. Kelly's 13th Cavalry Brigade. Kelly's brigade crossed the Samarian Hills on tracks so rough that in places the horses had to be led. At Jarak two squadrons of Hodson's Horse were detached to act as flank guard and at 02:15 a halt was called to allow the regiments to close up. Crossing the Plain of Esdraelon, the brigade began climbing the foothills towards Nazareth. Shortly after 04:00 it entered the village of El Mujeidel, where a delay occurred while part of the 18th Lancers rounded up a number sleeping Turks who might otherwise have sent a warning to Nazareth. The same process was repeated at Yafa, a mile and a half short of the objective, and more lancers were detached to escort the prisoners.

It was first light before the leading elements of the brigade reached a point south of the town, where a squadron of 18th Lancers was detached to cover the road from Afula. This became engaged almost immediately with a convoy of lorries heading for the town, escorted by some 400 Turks, who surrendered after a brief fight. One of the lorries carried a chest containing £20,000 in gold coin and notes; another, carrying petrol, was guarded by a huge bear, which made a great nuisance of itself. Sanders, it seems, was awakened by the shooting and, according to his housekeeper, made a hasty pyjama-clad exit in his car, a matter on which he subsequently declined to comment.

Kelly sent the remaining squadron of 18th Lancers to contain a large Turkish barracks while, with the Gloucesters and the few remaining lancers, he attempted to isolate the town from the north. At 04:25 the Gloucesters charged into the town, which now resembled a disturbed ant hill. Many Germans and Turks, unarmed and half-dazed with sleep, surrendered at once, but others were for making a fight of it. The German GHQ clerks in particular displayed desperate courage and managed to burn most of their papers before they were all but annihilated. Resistance continued to stiffen as Liman, now fully dressed,

Infantry and Indian animal tranport crossing the Turkish lines. On the right, a short convoy of wounded in camel litters passes in the opposite direction. Taken at 12:30 on 19 September. (IWM Neg Q12973)

returned to direct the fighting. At 06:50 Kelly sent a message to Macandrew requesting assistance from the 14th Cavalry Brigade; having taken 1,200 prisoners, his hands were more than full. In due course a reply was received saying that the horses were exhausted and that Kelly should withdraw in the direction of Afula. Shortly after 10:00 the Gloucesters, covered by Hodson's Horse and the 18th Lancers, broke contact. In the circumstances, casualties had been remarkably light. The Gloucesters lost two killed, 11 wounded, six missing and 28 horses killed, and Hodson's Horse two killed and nine wounded; the 18th Lancers' losses are unknown.

Despite Macandrew's comment regarding 14th Cavalry Brigade, the latter was already south of Nazareth and making for Afula when, at 06:30, the Poona Horse came across another convoy, consisting of seven lorries filled with Germans and Turks. A running fight ensued until the convoy ran into the covering squadron of 18th Lancers. Brigadier-general G. V. Clarke, commanding 14th Cavalry Brigade, then ordered up his machine gun squadron and the enemy surrendered, having first set fire to their vehicles. D Squadron The Poona Horse then encountered a column retreating from Afula which it promptly charged, killing several and taking over 200 prisoners.

Allenby, Chauvel and Macandrew were all bitterly disappointed that Kelly had failed to capture Sanders. Later, this would cost Kelly his job on the grounds of delay, depleting his force by dropping off too many squadrons, failure to isolate Nazareth before first light and the exhaustion of his horses. This was extremely harsh by any standards, but

BREAKTHROOUGH ON THE COASTAL SECTOR, 19 SEPTEMBER 1918
In the early morning of 19 September Bulfin's infantry moved forward quickly. On reaching the Turkish lines, now smothered under a pall of dust and smoke, the thin belt of wire was soon breached with planks, corrugated iron or stuffed sandbags. A flurry of grenades exploded around the parapets and then the attackers went in

with the bayonet. Most of the Turks were too stunned or confused by events to offer resistance and there were mass surrenders. Behind a carefully controlled creeping barrage, successive waves took up the advance to secure the second and reserve line of trenches, Leading squadrons of the Desert Mounted Corps followed up to break through and encircle the Turkish positions.

especially so when one considers the results of the raid. At 13:15 Sanders abandoned Nazareth and, accompanied by only three staff officers, drove to Tiberias then to Samakh at the southern end of Lake Tiberias (the Sea of Galilee), where he established a temporary GHQ during the evening. Thus the Yilderim Army Group was effectively deprived of its commander for the entire day.

Major-general Barrow's 4th Cavalry Division had been given the responsibility of securing the Musmus Pass. During the previous evening's rest period Barrow had issued orders that the division would continue its advance at 22:00, with Brigadier-general R. G. H. Howard-Vyse's 10th Cavalry Brigade leading. Speed was of the essence, since an officer prisoner had disclosed that an enemy force had already been detailed to block the pass. Howard-Vyse was ordered to send the 2nd Lancers, reinforced with two armoured cars of 11th LAMB and additional machine gunners, to the cross-roads at Ara, inside the pass, and the regiment moved off at 20:45. As both its commanding officer and second-in-command were ill, it was commanded by 30-year-old Captain D. S. Davison. Having captured 200 stragglers, who were sent back under escort, 2nd Lancers reached Ara at about 23:30 and took up position around the cross-roads.

ED '98

Meticulous planning ensured that even a portion of the heavy artillery was available to follow up the advance. Here a heavy howitzer is towed across firm going by a Holt tractor. (IWM Neg Q69761)

Two hours earlier, Barrow had called in on Howard-Vyse and was astonished to learn that the latter had ordered his brigade to move at 23:30 instead of 22:00 as specified in divisional orders. The reason given was that watering the horses was taking longer than had been expected. Seriously alarmed, Barrow told Howard-Vyse to move at 23:00 whether or not watering had been completed, and, accompanied by Lieutenant-colonel W. J. Foster, his GSO1, Barrow drove on to contact Davison. He then sent the armoured cars through the pass to verify that it was clear as far as Umm el Fahm, its northern entrance, and when they confirmed this, he sent the 2nd Lancers through.

Time passed without any sign of the rest of the brigade and Barrow decided to retrace his steps. Eventually he learned to his horror that 10th Cavalry Brigade had missed the entrance to the pass – an easy thing to do, especially at night, for while the interior of the pass is narrow and tortuous, the southern entrance is a flat expanse 300 yards wide set between very low hills. The 10th Cavalry Brigade was now some miles beyond, with divisional headquarters and part of 11th Cavalry Brigade following. After sending Colonel Foster to find the errant column, Barrow contacted Brigadier-general T. J. Wigan, commanding 12th Cavalry Brigade, at about 01:00 and told him to secure the pass, taking 2nd Lancers under command. Shortly afterwards, a staff officer from 10th Cavalry Brigade arrived to say that during its return journey the brigade had again missed the entrance to the pass and was off on another false trail. Barrow removed Howard-Vyse from his command on the spot, replacing him with Lieutenant-colonel W. G. K. Green of Jacob's Horse.

Davison's command reached El Lajjun (Megiddo) at the northern end of the pass at about 03:00 to find about 100 Turks, their arms piled, sitting round a fire, singing. They were the advance guard of Major Frey's force, sent by Sanders to defend the pass, and were too surprised to offer any resistance. The leading elements of 12th Cavalry Brigade emerged from the pass at about 04:30 and an hour later Wigan despatched 2nd Lancers, who had used the interval to water their horses and snatch breakfast, to capture Afula and cut the railway there.

Motor transport – in this case a convoy of Model T Fords – played a vital role in maintaining the momentum of the advance. (IWM Neg Q24370)

At 05:30 Davison's command was advancing along the Afula road on a three-squadron frontage when it came under fire from what was evidently a considerable Turkish force occupying a position in front of the village of Birket el Fuleh. Davison directed his centre squadron, 11th LAMB's armoured cars and the machine gunners to engage the enemy frontally while his reserve squadron, taking advantage of dead ground, charged the Turkish position from the right. On his own initiative the officer commanding the right squadron conformed to the attack. This brilliant little action lasted little more than five minutes and resulted in 46 Turks being speared and 470 captured. The lancers' casualties amounted to one man wounded and 12 horses killed. The Turks were the main body of Major Frey's force and no explanation exists as to why they had taken so long to march from Nazareth. Frey was not among the

The main street of Tul Karm, the day after it fell to the 60th Division. (IWM Neg Q12321)

prisoners, and later arrived in Samakh, where Sanders doubtless expressed his views on the defeat.

Resuming the advance, 2nd Lancers came under fire from Afula itself at 07:45. This, however, was short-lived, since the Deccan Horse of 5th Cavalry Division were already attacking the town and by 08:00 the enemy garrison – 75 Germans and 200 Turks – surrendered. Also captured were ten locomotives and 50 trucks, much petrol and a stock of champagne. Three aircraft were captured on the airfield and a fourth, carrying mail, was shot down as it came in to land. A convoy of 12 German lorries attempted to escape along the Beisan road but was run down by the armoured cars.

During the morning the 4th Cavalry Division concentrated at Afula. At 13:00 it resumed its advance along the Valley of Jezreel to Beisan, which was secured without difficulty by 18:00. Three 150mm howitzers were captured and several hundred prisoners; hundreds more came in during the night. The division had covered 70 miles in 34 hours, had secured all its objectives save one, and its weary horses could now rest.

The remaining objective was Jisr el Majami at the confluence of the Yarmuk with the Jordan. The 19th Lancers, reinforced with a section from the 18th Machine Gun Company and 4th Field Squadron RE, had spent the afternoon resting at Afula. At 19:30 the regiment set out on a rough cross-country march of 20 miles, reaching Jisr el Majami before first light next morning. The few Turks holding the railway fled, the bridges were prepared for demolition and rails removed from the track. The Palestine railway system was now isolated.

THE ESCAPE OF GENERAL LIMAN VON SANDERS FROM NAZARETH, 20 SEPTEMBER 1918.
The 5th Cavalry Division, with 12th LAMB and 7th LCP attached, was to continue northwards to Abu Shushe, where it was to send a detachment to Nazareth with the object of capturing Sanders' GHQ and, if possible, Sanders himself. The Gloucestershire Yeomanry came very close to capturing Sanders, but he pulled back and at 13:15 abandoned the town.

Nazareth, the location of the Turkish GHQ. The 13th Cavalry Brigade's attempt to capture General Liman von Sanders by *coup de main* failed narrowly. Sanders evacuated the town later the same day. (IWM Neg Q12349)

Meanwhile, Major-general H. W. Hodgson's Australian Mounted Division had also come into the picture. Hodgson, it will be recalled, had already detached 5th Light Horse Brigade to work with Shea's 60th Division. Now he had to break up the 4th Light Horse Brigade temporarily. One regiment was employed as escort to Corps HQ, another to escort the divisional transport and the third to convoy the 5th Cavalry Division's transport through the Musmus Pass. By the time he reached El Lajjun this left him with only Brigadier-general L. C. Wilson's 3rd Light Horse Brigade and divisional troops.

At 14:45 Chauvel received an air reconnaissance report to the effect that the enemy was retreating northwards in large numbers from Jenin, to the south of Afula. At 15:30 Hodgson, under Chauvel's direction, ordered Wilson to intercept the fugitives with 3rd Light Horse Brigade, less one regiment, which would remain at El Lajjun, reinforcing Wilson with 11th LAMB, now under corps control. The leading regiment, 10th Light Horse, commanded by Lieutenant-colonel A. C. N. Olden, had covered 11 miles in 70 minutes when, at Kufr Adan, three miles north-west of Jenin, a large body of the enemy – some 1,800 strong, including a number of Germans – was spotted in a grove, deployed as if to meet a British infantry attack from the south. 2nd Lieutenant P. W. K. Doig's troop immediately charged and the enemy, taken completely by surprise, surrendered at once.

Having detached a squadron to cut the Jenin–Zir'in road, the regiment made for the town. Save for brief resistance by some German

El Lajjun (Megiddo) seen from the northern exit of the Musmus Pass. The Plain of Esdraelon stretches towards Nazareth in the distant hills. Once the Desert Mounted Corps had reached this point the fate of the Yilderim Army Group was settled. (IWM Neg Q12975)

machine gunners, there was no opposition. By the light of burning supply dumps the townspeople emerged to throw themselves on the immense stores of food, clothing and equipment in a frenzy of looting. In the words of the official historian, the scene resembled the sack of a town during the Thirty Years War.

The 9th Light Horse had now come up, but the Australians were heavily outnumbered by the 3,000 prisoners they had taken and were hard pressed to restore order. However, another bullion wagon was rescued, together with 120 cases of German champagne.

During the night more and more retreating Turks, weary and demoralised, converged on Jenin. Most gave up willingly, and others were bluffed into surrender, so that by dawn Wilson's regiments found themselves guarding no fewer than 8,000 prisoners. Urgent messages to Hodgson resulted in him ordering forward two regiments of 4th Light Horse Brigade, which had reassembled at El Lajjun. During its march to the POW compound, the column was led by the Germans, who had retained their discipline and punctiliously goose-stepped whenever a car displaying a general's pennon approached.

Elsewhere during the day the British infantry divisions had drawn the steel net ever tighter around the Yilderim Army Group, especially in the west, where the 60th, 7th and 3rd divisions continued to exert inexorable pressure against its crumbling flank. The infantry's part in the battle was now all but over. XX Corps had sustained 1,505 casualties, including 225 killed; it had taken 6,851 prisoners, 140 guns and

Tel Megiddo, from which the battle took its name, as seen on the morning of 20 September. On the left the Staffordshire Yeomanry unsaddle briefly. On the right is the road to Afula and Nazareth. (IWM Neg Q12976)

1,345 machine guns and automatic rifles. XXI Corps' casualties amounted to 3,378, including 446 killed; by the end of the battle it had taken about 12,000 prisoners, 149 guns, 287 machine guns and automatic rifles and large quantities of stores.

Whatever chance Yilderim had had of containing the catastrophe vanished on 20 September. By noon the headquarters of Seventh and Eighth armies had begun to issue orders for a limited withdrawal, but as the day wore on it became clear that as the British cavalry progressively blocked all escape routes to the north, it would inevitably escalate into a general retreat across the Jordan fords.

THE CAPTURE OF MUSMUS PASS, 21 SEPTEMBER 1918 Major-general Barrow's 4th Cavalry Division had been given the responsibility of securing the Musmus Pass. The 2nd Lancers, under the command of 30-year-old Captain D. S. Davison, were to lead the assault. Davison's command reached El Lajjun

(Megiddo) at the northern end of the pass at about 03:00 to find about 100 Turks, their arms piled, sitting round a fire, singing. They were the advance guard of Major Frey's force, sent by Sanders to defend the pass, and were too surprised to offer any resistance

During the evening Colonel von Oppen received orders from Mustapha Kemal for the Asia Korps to cover the retreat of the Seventh Army. Kemal had no authority to issue orders direct to a formation of Eighth Army, albeit that the Asia Korps was one of the latter's few remnants; Oppen chose to disregard them.

At midnight Sanders left Samakh for Deraa. His immediate plan was to form an L-shaped holding line behind which his troops could rally once they were across the Jordan. This would stretch southwards from Lake Hula down the Jordan valley to Samakh on Lake Tiberias and then east to Deraa. Thus far Djemal Kuçuk's Fourth Army had not been directly affected by the disaster, although it had been subjected to air attack, and Arab raids against the Hejaz railway had intensified. However, Djemal had received no instructions from Sanders for two days and had thus lost any reasonable chance of extracting his II Corps from Ma'an, far to the south, although orders for it to move had been given. It became clear that what remained of the Yilderim Army Group would be retiring on Damascus, covered by the Fourth Army.

21 September

This was a relatively quiet day, during which Nazareth was occupied and a major part of the Seventh Army, retreating along the Wadi Far'a, was destroyed by the RAF. The long column was spotted at dawn and its head was attacked first, bringing it to a standstill. The attacks continued all day, two aircraft appearing every three minutes to bomb and strafe, and an additional six every half-hour. For two miles the road was choked with wrecked and abandoned vehicles and guns. At one point lorry drivers had tried to batter their way through, smashing into guns, carts and their teams until the accumulation of wreckage and dead animals brought the avalanche to a halt. At another, where the road ran along a ledge, guns and vehicles had been swept over the edge to crash into the stream below.

Curiously, very few of the enemy had been killed; most had succumbed to blind terror and fled into the hills, from which they were winkled out in due course. It took several days to extract about 100 guns from the wreckage, and in some places the tangle was so bad that it could only be cleared by burning. This was the first occasion in history when a major formation was virtually annihilated by air power alone.

The Asia Korps, together with elements of the Turkish 16th and 19th divisions, was now acting as Sanders' rearguard. During 21 September the remnants of the 702nd and 703rd battalions were amalgamated to form a single weak battalion consisting of one rifle company, one machine gun company and a trench-mortar detachment. On learning that the Wadi Far'a was blocked, Colonel von Oppen decided to try for the ford at Jisr el Damiya.

Some of the Turkish prisoners captured at Beisan. In the right foreground the seated officer with the white armband is the GOC of the Turkish 16th Division. (IWM Neg Q12977)

The railway bridge at Jisr el Majami, where the Jordan and Yarmuk rivers meet, was secured intact by 19th Lancers. (IWM Neg Q12980)

22 September

Chaytor's force captured Jisr el Damiya at about 13:00. Now all but trapped, Oppen ordered his German troops to abandon their baggage and guns and make their way over Mount Ebal. In so doing they attracted artillery fire but escaped with little loss. By now Oppen's strength had been reduced to 700 Germans and 1,300 Turks, but he believed that he could break through to Samakh by attacking Beisan during the night, a course of action favoured by Sanders. In all probability the attempt would have failed, but at this point Djevad Pasha, still Oppen's immediate superior, quashed the idea and ordered him to cross the Jordan at the ford of Makhadet Abu Naj, which he did immediately, getting all his German and most of his Turkish troops across before it came under attack.

Sanders, meanwhile, had received a signal from the German Military Mission in Constantinople – which clearly had not the slightest idea what was going on – requesting him to present a prize for the sack-race in a forthcoming military sports meeting. Sanders commented dryly that he was not interested in sports, least of all in a sack-race – a painful reminder of his own position!

Understandably, Allenby's mood was in complete contrast when he strode into HQ Desert Mounted Corps at El Lajjun that morning. Chauvel told him that he had some 15,000 prisoners for him. 'No bloody good to me!' replied the army commander, 'I want 30,000 from you before you've done!' He then announced that the beaten enemy would be pursued to Damascus and that to ease the logistic aspects of the

Australian 5th Light Horse Brigade, together with Spahis and Chasseurs d'Afrique, entering Nablus on 21 September. (IWM Neg Q12330)

DESTRUCTION OF THE TURKISH 7TH ARMY IN WADI FAR'A

The long column of the Turkish 7th Army was spotted at dawn and its head was attacked first, bringing it to a standstill. The attacks continued all day, two aircraft appearing every three minutes to bomb and strafe, and an additional six every half-hour. For two miles the road was choked with wrecked and abandoned vehicles and guns. Very few of the enemy were killed; most fled into the hills. It took several days to extract about 100 guns from the wreckage, and in some places the tangle was so bad that it could only be cleared by burning. This was the first occasion in history when a major formation was virtually annihilated by air power alone.

operation the port of Haifa was to be captured. Elsewhere air reconnaissance had revealed that large numbers of the enemy were escaping across the Jordan by the Makhadet Abu Naj and other nearby fords, and it was decided to close this gap.

23 September

Chauvel gave the task of capturing Haifa to 5th Cavalry Division, adding the port of Acre, 12 miles to the north, to its list of objectives, and detailed 4th Cavalry Division to close the Jordan fords.

Acre was taken without undue difficulty by the 13th Cavalry Brigade, but Haifa, the objective of Brigadier-general C. R. Harbord's 15th Cavalry Brigade, proved to be a much tougher nut to crack. This was partly because its garrison had not been directly affected by the general Turkish collapse and partly because the direct approach to the town lay along a narrow neck of land between Mount Carmel Ridge to the south and the river Kishon (Nahr el Muqatta) to the north. Harbord was further handicapped by having had to detach the Hyderabad Lancers to escort prisoners, leaving him with only the Jodhpore and Mysore Lancers, supported by B Battery HAC.

The brigade's advance guard was engaged by machine guns firing from north of the river and the northern slopes of Mount Carmel, and by artillery positioned near a religious establishment, the Karmelheim, at the western end of the ridge. Harbord mounted a three-pronged attack, timed to go in at 14:00. One squadron of Mysore Lancers was detached to attack the enemy north of the river while another, supported by the Sherwood Rangers from 14th Cavalry Brigade, who had arrived at 11:50, was to follow a track along the summit of Mount Carmel and charge the guns. In the centre the two remaining Mysore squadrons would provide fire support for a charge by the Jodhpore Lancers along the neck of land and into the town.

The Jodhpores' approach was complicated by the nature of the Kishon: two of their ground scouts were swallowed immediately in quicksand. The regiment's leading squadron was promptly ordered to swing left and charge the machine gunners on Carmel's lower slopes, which it did successfully. This opened the defile for the rest of the regiment to charge into the town along the road and railway, followed by the Mysore fire-support squadrons. The simultaneous attack north of the river had also succeeded.

On Mount Carmel itself the Mysore squadron made a difficult ascent, losing horses from exhaustion, lameness and enemy fire, so that when the moment came for the attack, only 15 mounted men remained. These nevertheless executed a charge over broken, stony ground, supported by two machine guns and the squadron's Hotchkiss section from a flank. They captured a 150mm naval gun, two mountain guns and 78 prisoners. At this moment the first of the Sherwood Rangers arrived to follow through with the pursuit, and captured a further 50 Turks.

This brilliant action, which could so easily have ended badly, had been won by the speed, aggression and professionalism of those involved. Altogether, two naval, four 4.2in., six 77mm and four 10-pdr. camel guns were taken, as well as 10 machine guns, a large quantity of ammunition and stores, and numerous – very welcome – fresh horses. Casualties included Lieutenant-colonel Thakur Dalpat Singh,

No less than 8,000 prisoners were captured by the Australian 3rd Light Horse Brigade at Jenin. The Germans leading the column on its way to the prisoner of war compounds invariably paid the correct compliments to every general's car that passed. (IWM Neg Q12339)

Some of the vehicles captured by the Australians at Jenin. Visible are various types of cart, limbers and water wagons. In the foreground are two German field kitchens, known familiarly as 'goulasch cannons'. (IWM Neg Q12347)

On 21 September the bulk of the Turkish Seventh Army was destroyed by sustained air attack while it retreated along the Wadi Far'a. This photograph, taken after the worst of the tangle had been sorted out, shows horse-drawn guns, limbers, wagons and even a private *gharri*.
(IWM Neg Q12310)

commanding the Jodhpore Lancers, and two others killed, 34 wounded, 64 horses killed and 83 horses wounded. Four days later the first supplies were landed at Haifa.

Major-general Barrow had detailed the 11th Cavalry Brigade, under Brigadier-general Gregory, to close the remaining Jordan fords. The brigade advanced down both banks of the river, meeting varying degrees of opposition. Some of the Turks, believing themselves to be within sight of safety, fought very hard, especially at Makhadet Abu Naj, where the fire of some concealed guns temporarily silenced the Hants Battery RHA. As always, movement around a flank proved to be the answer and four of the enemy's guns were captured in a charge by C Squadron, the Middlesex Yeomanry. Nowhere would the Turks stand against a mounted charge.

The operation continued overnight and into the next day until the ground around the fords, and the routes to and from them, were littered with the enemy dead and over 9,000 prisoners had been taken. During the night a 29th Lancer patrol made contact with the Worcestershire Yeomanry, the cavalry regiment of XX Corps.

To the south Chaytor's force, led by the New Zealand Mounted Rifles Brigade, had advanced into trans-Jordan and by 18:30 had taken Es Salt. The following morning, having been ordered by Allenby to stop the Turks retiring northwards from Amman, Chaytor despatched 100 men of the Auckland Mounted Rifles to destroy a section of the Hejaz railway five miles north of the town.

THE CAPTURE OF HAIFA

23 September 1918

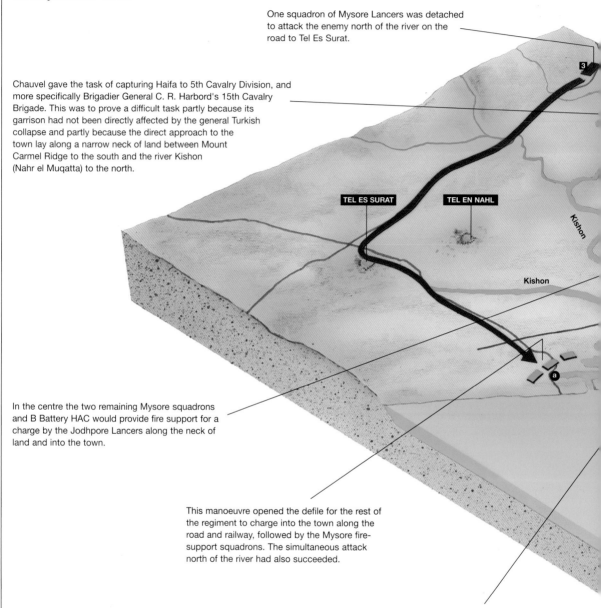

One squadron of Mysore Lancers was detached to attack the enemy north of the river on the road to Tel Es Surat.

Chauvel gave the task of capturing Haifa to 5th Cavalry Division, and more specifically Brigadier General C. R. Harbord's 15th Cavalry Brigade. This was to prove a difficult task partly because its garrison had not been directly affected by the general Turkish collapse and partly because the direct approach to the town lay along a narrow neck of land between Mount Carmel Ridge to the south and the river Kishon (Nahr el Muqatta) to the north.

In the centre the two remaining Mysore squadrons and B Battery HAC would provide fire support for a charge by the Jodhpore Lancers along the neck of land and into the town.

This manoeuvre opened the defile for the rest of the regiment to charge into the town along the road and railway, followed by the Mysore fire-support squadrons. The simultaneous attack north of the river had also succeeded.

The Jodhpores' approach was complicated by nature of the Kishon: two of their ground scouts were swallowed immediately in quicksand. The regiment's leading squadron was promptly ordered to swing left and charge the machine gunners on Carmel's lower slopes, which it did successfully.

TEL ES SURAT

TEL EN NAHL

Kishon

Kishon

EGYPTIAN EXPEDITIONARY FORCE UNITS	CENTRAL POWER'S UNITS
1 15th Cavalry Brigade	**a** Turkish Depot Regiment
2 1 Sqn. Mysore Lancers	**b** Machine gun Company and assorted artillery
3 1 Sqn. Mysore Lancers	
4 2 Sqns. Mysore Lancers	
5 Jodhpore Lancers	
6 B Battery HAC	

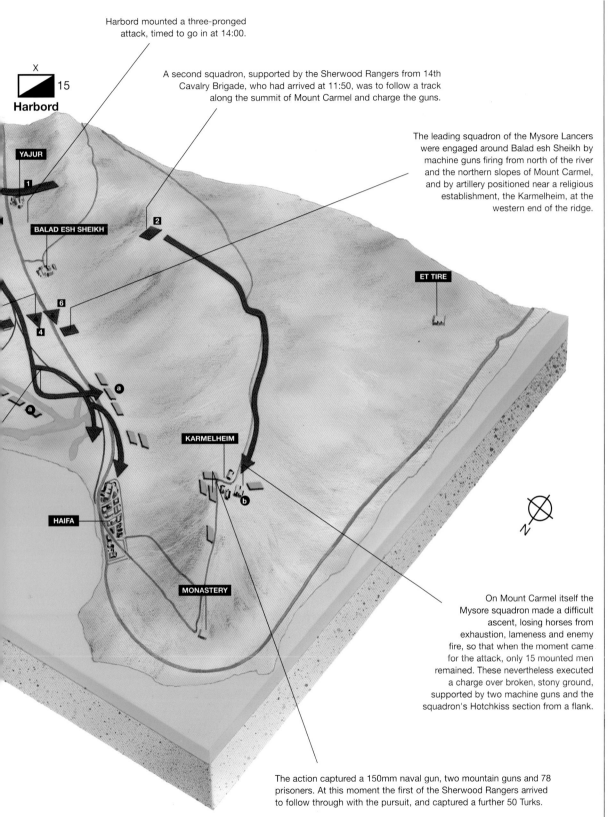

Harbord mounted a three-pronged attack, timed to go in at 14:00.

A second squadron, supported by the Sherwood Rangers from 14th Cavalry Brigade, who had arrived at 11:50, was to follow a track along the summit of Mount Carmel and charge the guns.

The leading squadron of the Mysore Lancers were engaged around Balad esh Sheikh by machine guns firing from north of the river and the northern slopes of Mount Carmel, and by artillery positioned near a religious establishment, the Karmelheim, at the western end of the ridge.

X

15

Harbord

YAJUR

1

BALAD ESH SHEIKH

2

ET TIRE

6

4

a

a

KARMELHEIM

b

HAIFA

MONASTERY

On Mount Carmel itself the Mysore squadron made a difficult ascent, losing horses from exhaustion, lameness and enemy fire, so that when the moment came for the attack, only 15 mounted men remained. These nevertheless executed a charge over broken, stony ground, supported by two machine guns and the squadron's Hotchkiss section from a flank.

The action captured a 150mm naval gun, two mountain guns and 78 prisoners. At this moment the first of the Sherwood Rangers arrived to follow through with the pursuit, and captured a further 50 Turks.

Another view of the destruction wrought by the RAF in the Wadi Far'a. This was the first occasion in history when a major formation was wiped out by air power alone. Comparatively few Turks were killed, most having escaped into the hills. (IWM Neg Q12311)

25 September

The Turkish Seventh and Eighth armies had now ceased to exist and all of Palestine west of the Jordan, save for Samakh, was in British hands. Samakh was the hinge of the holding line Sanders was struggling to construct and he had reinforced the garrison there with German machine gunners, ordering the commandant, Captain von Keyserling, to hold to the last man.

The town was attacked before dawn by Brigadier-general W. Grant's 4th Australian Light Horse Brigade (ALH), which the previous year had carried out an epic charge at Beersheba. On this occasion, however, Grant's numbers were seriously depleted, since 4th ALH was guarding Chauvel's headquarters and five troops of 12th ALH were escorting prisoners. Grant had been promised reinforcements but rather than wait for these to arrive and lose the benefit of darkness, he ordered 11th ALH to make a mounted attack across open ground from the south-east, covered by machine gun fire. The 12th ALH he held in reserve.

At 04:25 the light horse regiment, commanded by Lieutenant-colonel J. W. Parsons, charged with drawn swords in two lines of half-squadrons, with about 200 yards between lines, yelling so as to indicate their position to the supporting machine gunners. Men and horses began to go down to the enemy's return fire, but Australians broke through the eastern defences and, sheathing their swords, went in with the rifle and bayonet. In the words of the Official History:

'Dawn came up on one of the hottest and most fiercely contested fights of the whole campaign as the two Australian squadrons assaulted the station buildings. The enemy lined a stout stone wall, fired automatic rifles from the windows, hurled bombs. Several parties had established themselves in engines and tenders in the sidings. The struggle raged a full hour, quarter being neither asked nor given, until every man of the defenders had been killed or wounded. In the village

Worcestershire Yeomanry, the cavalry regiment of XX Corps, passing through the Wadi Far'a. Local looters are already in evidence. (IWM Neg Q12308)

itself, where a squadron of 12th ALH took part, afterwards moving on for the final stages of the battle for the station, the fighting was less severe, and here a number of prisoners were taken. By 05:30 it was all over. Two motor-boats lying at the jetty made off in the midst of the action but one was caught by a burst of fire from a Hotchkiss rifle, broke into flames, and sank.'

About 100 Germans were killed. Among the 364 prisoners taken were some 200 Turks who had played little part in the fighting. One gun, ten machine guns, an aircraft and a quantity of rolling stock were captured. The Australians' casualties amounted to 78 killed and wounded; they also lost nearly 100 horses, most of which were killed.

Grant now ordered one squadron of 12th ALH to move up the western shore of the lake towards Tiberias. In so doing it encountered a squadron of 8th ALH and the 12th LAMB and the combined force pushed on to occupy the town against slight opposition, taking nearly 100 prisoners and 13 machine guns.

Across the Jordan, Chaytor's ANZAC Mounted Division had continued its advance from Es Salt to Amman. At about 10:40 an aircraft dropped a message to the effect that the garrison was pulling out. The Turkish rearguard, however, continued to offer stiff resistance. A mounted attack by the Canterbury Mounted Rifles was stopped by machine gun fire from the Citadel, but the regiment dismounted and cleared the position with the bayonet. Simultaneously, Brigadier-general G. de L. Ryrie's 2nd Light Horse Brigade, having cleared some sangars, fought its way into the town, where resistance suddenly collapsed at about 13:30. Captures included 2,563 prisoners, ten guns, numerous machine guns, 300 horses and considerable quantities of forage.

In waiting so long for the arrival of his II Corps from Ma'an, Djemal Kuçuk had fatally delayed the withdrawal of the rest of the Fourth Army, since the railway, thanks to the depredations of Chaytor's force and the

Arabs, was now inoperable as far north as Deraa. Most of his men faced a long, thirsty march with the ever-present danger of the Arabs hovering on their flank, knowing that the latter would show no mercy to stragglers or the wounded. The Battle of Megiddo was over; the final ejection of the Turks from Palestine and Syria was about to begin.

THE SITUATION AT 9PM, 24 SEPTEMBER 1918

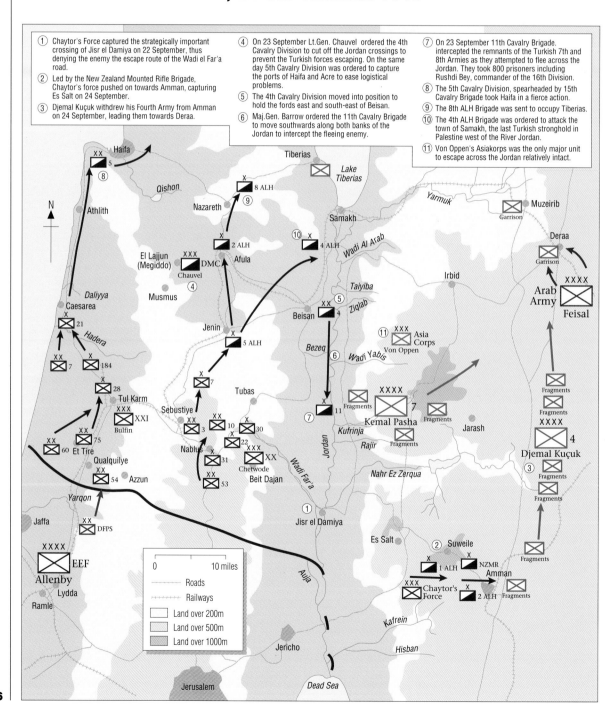

1. Chaytor's Force captured the strategically important crossing of Jisr el Damiya on 22 September, thus denying the enemy the escape route of the Wadi el Far'a road.

2. Led by the New Zealand Mounted Rifle Brigade, Chaytor's force pushed on towards Amman, capturing Es Salt on 24 September.

3. Djemal Kuçuk withdrew his Fourth Army from Amman on 24 September, leading them towards Deraa.

4. On 23 September Lt.Gen. Chauvel ordered the 4th Cavalry Division to cut off the Jordan crossings to prevent the Turkish forces escaping. On the same day 5th Cavalry Division was ordered to capture the ports of Haifa and Acre to ease logistical problems.

5. The 4th Cavalry Division moved into position to hold the fords east and south-east of Beisan.

6. Maj.Gen. Barrow ordered the 11th Cavalry Brigade to move southwards along both banks of the Jordan to intercept the fleeing enemy.

7. On 23 September 11th Cavalry Brigade, intercepted the remnants of the Turkish 7th and 8th Armies as they attempted to flee across the Jordan. They took 800 prisoners including Rushdi Bey, commander of the 16th Division.

8. The 5th Cavalry Division, spearheaded by 15th Cavalry Brigade took Haifa in a fierce action.

9. The 8th ALH Brigade was sent to occupy Tiberias.

10. The 4th ALH Brigade was ordered to attack the town of Samakh, the last Turkish stronghold in Palestine west of the River Jordan.

11. Von Oppen's Asiakorps was the only major unit to escape across the Jordan relatively intact.

Officers examine an abandoned Turkish field gun. The ammunition boxes seem to be made of wicker rather than wood. (IWM Neg Q12319)

The Road to Damascus 26 September – 1 October

Allenby had set Damascus and Beirut as his next objectives and so brought XXI Corps back into the picture. The 7th Division relieved the 5th Cavalry Division at Haifa, the 3rd Division moved up through Jenin and Nazareth to Samakh and the 54th Division began marching north on the coastal sector. Within the Desert Mounted Corps the Australian Mounted Division and the 5th Cavalry Division were to concentrate at Tiberias and Nazareth respectively and then, with the Australian Mounted Division leading, were to cross the Jordan at Jisr Benat Yukub (the Bridge of the Daughters of Jacob) between Lakes Hula and Tiberias, and advance through Kuneitra to Damascus. They were to arrive on the morning of 28 September; the 4th Cavalry Division was to march on Deraa, co-operate with the Arab army attacking the railway, then proceed northward along the Pilgrims' road, through Kiswe to Damascus; all were to march light and live off the country as much as possible.

Park of equipment captured from the Turkish Seventh Army, including 101 guns. There were over 87 guns, 55 lorries, four cars and 932 horse-drawn vehicles found wrecked or abandoned in a five-mile stretch of the Wadi Far'a. (IWM Neg Q12341)

Very few options remained open to Liman von Sanders. He had reached Damascus during the evening of 23 September and, recognising that the city was not defensible, had finally re-established his GHQ at Ba'albek. He requested reinforcements from the commander of Second Army but the latter was only able to spare a few battalions. Sanders was relying heavily on an ad hoc collection of troops, known as the Tiberias Group, to hold the line of the Jordan between Lakes Hula and Tiberias and to retire stubbornly and prevent the British cutting in on the line of Turkish retreat through Deraa to Damascus. In the longer term he decided to establish a new front covering the railway junction at Riyaq. On 27 September he ordered Colonel von Oppen and the remnants of the Asia Korps to withdraw by train from Deraa. Nine hours had to be spent repairing a 500-yard breach in the line, but the train reached Damascus the next morning and went straight through to Riyaq.

There were also a number of changes in command. Mustapha Kemal was placed in command of the new front forming at Riyaq; Djemal Kuçuk, while retaining command of the Fourth Army, also took over the Tiberias Group and therefore became responsible for the Turkish withdrawal through Damascus; and Djevad Pasha was sent back to Constantinople, together with the staff of Eighth Army.

The Arab army was now in full cry and would play an important part in the coming operations. Its small regular element maintained its discipline, but the Turkish retreat provoked a general rising of the desert tribes, who were almost beyond control. As the Turks withdrew along the railway, they killed, raped and pillaged their way through one Arab village after another, sometimes committing the most bestial atrocities; at Tafas, not content with killing the women and children, they also indulged in mutilation. Naturally the Arabs wanted revenge, and whenever they overran a group of Turks, they indulged in an orgy of slaughter. In the midst of one of these scenes of carnage, Lawrence observed the conduct of the German 146th Regiment with a mixture of admiration and pity: 'They were 2,000 miles from home, without hope and without guides, in conditions mad enough to break the strongest nerves. Yet their sections held together in firm rank, sheering through the wreck of Turk and Arab like armoured ships, high-faced and silent.

Bird's-eye view of Haifa, taken on 23 September, the day of its dramatic capture by the Jodhpore and Mysore Lancers, 15th (Imperial Service) Cavalry Brigade, supported by B Battery HAC. (IWM Neg Q12336)

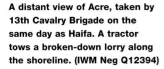
The Johdpore and Mysore Lancers leaving Haifa. Some of the troopers wear steel helmets, in a few cases with neck cloths, while others, for religious reasons, have retained their turbans. (IWM Neg Q12334)

When attacked, they halted, took position, fired to order. There was no haste, no crying, no hesitation.'

On the morning of 26 September the 4th Cavalry Division, led by 10th Cavalry Brigade, began its march on Deraa. During the afternoon the leading regiment, 2nd Lancers, now commanded by Major G. Gould, emerged from a defile to come under fire from two villages, El Bahira, on its left, and Irbid, situated on a ridge ahead. The first was quickly taken at a gallop, and Major Gould, wishing to secure water by nightfall, mounted a left flank attack on Irbid with three squadrons. This he did without proper reconnaissance and without waiting for the rest of the brigade to come up. A few men penetrated the village but they were driven out; the attack foundered with the loss of 12 killed, 30 wounded and many more horses lost. This was the first real check Chauvel's corps had sustained since the offensive began, and it stemmed from understandable over-confidence. The Turks, in fact, belonged to the Fourth Army and were the flank guard put out by Djemal Kuçuk while his troops passed through Deraa; not having been involved in the earlier disaster, their morale was unshaken. During the night they withdrew, leaving behind nine tons of barley and a small herd of cattle.

Next morning the advance was continued. The Dorset Yeomanry, now leading, came up with the Turks at the village of El Remte. When the leading troop deployed for dismounted action, some 300 of the

A distant view of Acre, taken by 13th Cavalry Brigade on the same day as Haifa. A tractor tows a broken-down lorry along the shoreline. (IWM Neg Q12394)

SAMAKH

25 September 1918

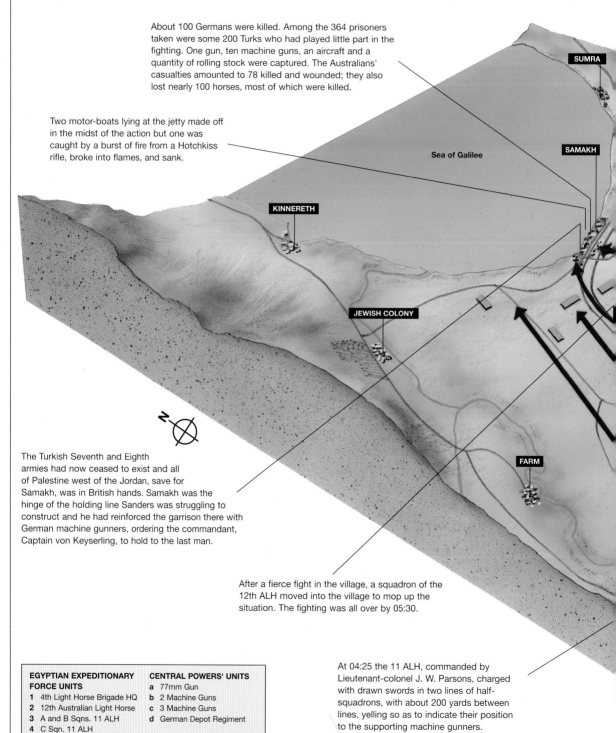

About 100 Germans were killed. Among the 364 prisoners taken were some 200 Turks who had played little part in the fighting. One gun, ten machine guns, an aircraft and a quantity of rolling stock were captured. The Australians' casualties amounted to 78 killed and wounded; they also lost nearly 100 horses, most of which were killed.

Two motor-boats lying at the jetty made off in the midst of the action but one was caught by a burst of fire from a Hotchkiss rifle, broke into flames, and sank.

SUMRA

SAMAKH

Sea of Galilee

KINNERETH

JEWISH COLONY

N

The Turkish Seventh and Eighth armies had now ceased to exist and all of Palestine west of the Jordan, save for Samakh, was in British hands. Samakh was the hinge of the holding line Sanders was struggling to construct and he had reinforced the garrison there with German machine gunners, ordering the commandant, Captain von Keyserling, to hold to the last man.

FARM

After a fierce fight in the village, a squadron of the 12th ALH moved into the village to mop up the situation. The fighting was all over by 05:30.

EGYPTIAN EXPEDITIONARY FORCE UNITS		CENTRAL POWERS' UNITS	
1	4th Light Horse Brigade HQ	a	77mm Gun
2	12th Australian Light Horse	b	2 Machine Guns
3	A and B Sqns. 11 ALH	c	3 Machine Guns
4	C Sqn. 11 ALH	d	German Depot Regiment
5	1 Troop, C Sqn. 11 ALH		
6	Machine Gun Sqn. 11 ALH		

At 04:25 the 11 ALH, commanded by Lieutenant-colonel J. W. Parsons, charged with drawn swords in two lines of half-squadrons, with about 200 yards between lines, yelling so as to indicate their position to the supporting machine gunners.

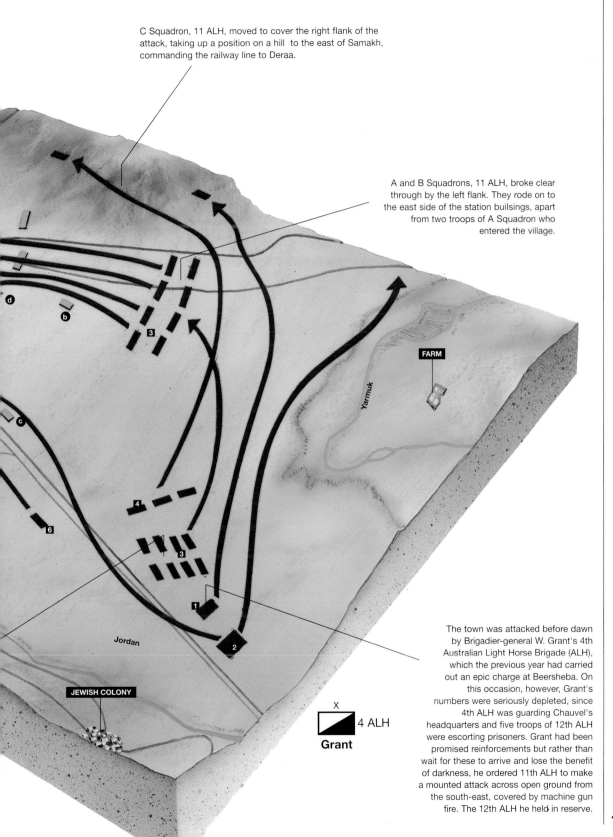

C Squadron, 11 ALH, moved to cover the right flank of the attack, taking up a position on a hill to the east of Samakh, commanding the railway line to Deraa.

A and B Squadrons, 11 ALH, broke clear through by the left flank. They rode on to the east side of the station buildsings, apart from two troops of A Squadron who entered the village.

FARM

Yarmuk

d

b

3

c

4

6

3

1

2

Jordan

JEWISH COLONY

X

4 ALH

Grant

The town was attacked before dawn by Brigadier-general W. Grant's 4th Australian Light Horse Brigade (ALH), which the previous year had carried out an epic charge at Beersheba. On this occasion, however, Grant's numbers were seriously depleted, since 4th ALH was guarding Chauvel's headquarters and five troops of 12th ALH were escorting prisoners. Grant had been promised reinforcements but rather than wait for these to arrive and lose the benefit of darkness, he ordered 11th ALH to make a mounted attack across open ground from the south-east, covered by machine gun fire. The 12th ALH he held in reserve.

The 1st Australian Light
Car Patrol on the coast road
near Mount Carmel.
(IWM Neg Q12323)

enemy, over-confident in their turn, mounted a counter-attack with the support of four machine guns. This dissolved into flight when the rest of the Dorsets arrived. One squadron of the Central India Horse joined in the pursuit, which overwhelmed the rest of the Turkish flank guard as it marched towards Deraa, taking several hundred more prisoners and eight machine guns. Because the horses were extremely tired and he was uncertain who held Deraa, Barrow halted for the rest of the day a few miles from the town.

On the morning of 28 September patrols reported fires in the station and it became clear that the Arabs had taken Deraa the previous afternoon. Barrow rode in with 10th Cavalry Brigade and was met with sights 'ghastly beyond aught that any man had yet witnessed'. Everywhere there were dead Turks, but they were the fortunate ones; for the wounded lay scattered about, despoiled and in agony, amid a litter of packages, half looted, half burnt, of torn documents, and smashed machinery. A long ambulance train full of sick and wounded Turks was drawn up in the station; the driver and fireman were still in their cab, still alive but mortally wounded. The Arabs were going through the train tearing off the clothing of the groaning and stricken Turks, regardless of gaping wounds and broken limbs, and cutting their victims' throats. The Arabs were pitched off the train, which was placed under British guard. The event was notable for a meeting between Barrow and Lawrence, each of whom took an instant dislike to the other. With the exception of its II Corps, Djemal Kuçuk's Fourth Army had made good its escape and for the next few days the 4th Cavalry Division would co-operate with the Arabs during the pursuit to Damascus.

The fate of the Turkish II Corps was decided that same day. An aircraft informed Chaytor that it had been

Colonel T. E. Lawrence. The
advance on Damascus involved
close co-operation with the Arab
army, which harried the Turkish
withdrawal along the Hejaz
Railway. (IWM Neg Q12629)

located at Ziza and a message was dropped to the enemy corps commander, Ali Bey Wakaby, demanding his surrender since all available water sources were now in British hands, and threatening air attack if he did not comply. The Turks agreed at once, but declined to lay down their arms until the arrival of a British force large enough to protect them from swarms of savage Arabs surrounding them.

Brigadier-general Ryrie's 2nd Light Horse Brigade was despatched to join the Turks, who were allowed to retain their weapons and actually outnumbered the Australians by eight to one. The Arabs, who were not part of Feisal's army, made several attacks during the night but the Turks beat them off, encouraged by Australian yells of 'Go on Jacko! Give it to the bastards!' The next morning the New Zealand Mounted Rifles Brigade arrived to guard the sick and wounded until they could be moved by train while Ryrie, having removed the rifle bolts of all save two Anatolian battalions, marched the remaining 4,000 prisoners into Amman.

Chaytor's force had now completed its task. It had taken 10,322 prisoners, 57 guns, 11 locomotives, a large quantity of rolling stock and much else besides at a cost of 27 killed, 105 wounded and seven missing. Having spent so long in the hot, humid lower Jordan valley, the men were beginning to suffer from the cold nights of the Arabian plateau. Outbreaks of disease, especially malaria, began to ravage the force, and they were later withdrawn to Jerusalem and Bethlehem to recover.

Meanwhile, the main thrust on Damascus had begun on the morning of 27 September. The now complete Australian Mounted Division, in the lead, found the bridge at Jisr Benat Yakub partially demolished and the far bank of the Jordan held in strength by an enemy force under the redoubtable Captain von Keyserling. Hard dismounted fighting followed, until the discovery of alternative fords enabled regiments to cross the river overnight. By then the enemy had decamped in motor lorries. Filing up the Golan Heights, the Australians reached Kuneitra at 13:00 on 28 September. The town itself might be displaying more white sheets than 'a Chinese laundry on a Monday', but as the area contained a large Circassian population who were pro-Turkish and potentially hostile, Chauvel formed a composite brigade under Brigadier-general Grant to protect his lines of communication. This consisted of 11th and

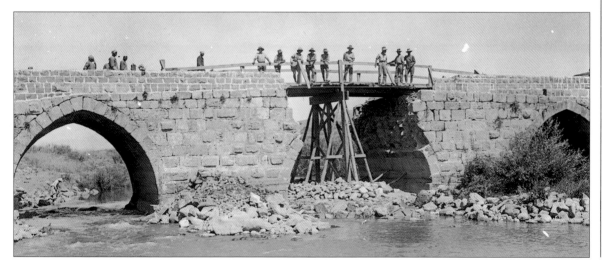

Turkish demolition temporarily held up the 5th Cavalry Division at Jisr Benat Yakub (the Bridge of the Daughters of Jacob), but the damage was quickly repaired by the 2nd Field Squadron, Australian Engineers.
(IWM Neg Q12352)

DERAA STATION , 28 SEPTEMBER 1918

On the morning of the 28th Barrow rode into Deraa with 10th Cavalry Brigade and was met with a horrendous sight. A long ambulance train full of sick and wounded Turks was drawn up in the station; the driver and fireman were still in their cab, alive but mortally wounded. The Arabs were going through

the train tearing off the clothing of the groaning and stricken Turks, regardless of gaping wounds and broken limbs, and cutting their victims' throats. The Arabs were pitched off the train, which was placed under British guard. The event was notable for a meeting between Barrow and Lawrence, each of whom took an instant dislike to the other.

DERAA

In the Barada Gorge, through which passed the westward road, railway and telegraph line from Damascus, the remnants of the Turkish Fourth Army was trapped and destroyed by elements of the Australian Mounted Division, firing from the heights above. The troop train yielded 480 prisoners. (IWM Neg Q12356)

15th ALH, the Sherwood Rangers and the Hyderabad Lancers, plus groups of men who were already dismounted or whose horses were showing signs of foundering.

During the morning of 29 September the armoured cars of 11th LAMB came up with the Turkish rearguard near Sa'sa. They were deployed across the road on rising ground covered with boulders and their left flank was protected by a lava field containing numerous wide crevasses. The Turks had pre-registered targets for their machine guns, the fire of which remained extremely accurate, even after dusk. Brigadier-general Wilson's 3rd Light Horse Brigade remained stalled until nightfall, when 9th and 10th ALH began the slow process of outflanking the position over difficult going. By 02:00 the next day it was

Part of the tangle of wreckage in the Barada Gorge. Among the vehicles were found 370 Turkish and German dead, eight guns and 30 machine guns. (IWM Neg Q12360)

apparent that the flanking moves were beginning to take effect. Wilson ordered the 8th ALH to make a dismounted attack straight up the road, and by 03:15 the position had been taken, together with seven machine guns. Once again, most of the enemy escaped in lorries.

As the day wore on the thump of guns to the east indicated that Barrow's 4th Cavalry Division was pushing the Fourth Army's rearguard steadily back on Damascus. Those Turks still opposing Hodgson's Australians were clearly unsettled and more willing to surrender. At Kaukab, 11 miles short of Damascus, a large body of them, holding a strong position, simply fled when Hodgson mounted a full divisional attack, a spectacle never likely to be seen again. Simultaneously, 5th Cavalry Division had come up on the right, intercepting and capturing most of a 2,000-strong column at Kiswe.

Djemal Kuçuk's fugitive Fourth Army was now streaming through Damascus in two directions – northwards along the road to Homs and westwards through the Barada Gorge towards Riyaq and Beirut. At about 16:30 elements of the Australian Mounted Division, led by the French Régiment Mixte and the 2nd New Zealand Machine Gun Squadron, reached the cliffs on the southern edge of the 100-yard-wide gorge and opened fire on the thousands of troops, transport vehicles and railway trains below. Two miles to the west the 9th ALH also reached the edge of the gorge and did likewise. The results are described in the Official History:

'The wretched Turks, seeing that to go forward meant complete destruction, turned back, only to fall into the hands of 14th ALH (which had closed in on the eastern end of the gorge). About four thousand prisoners were taken here . . . The enemy, or at least the Germans in his ranks, attempted resistance, but his situation was hopeless. Some struggled through, others turned back, while the Australians fired and fired till the road was littered with the bodies of men and animals and the wreckage of transport wagons. Four hundred dead were later found on

Kadem Station, Damascus, the terminus of the Hejaz railway. Turkish attempts to burn the rolling stock before they left were only half-hearted. (IWM Neg Q12371)

the road, and it took several days to burn the vehicles in order to clear the pass.'

It was impossible to cut the Homs road without passing through Damascus, but that night the city's military governor, Ali Riza Pasha el Rikabi, deserted and rode into the lines of 4th Cavalry Division. An Arab by birth, he had spent 40 years in the Turkish army but was now only too pleased to turn the tables on his masters, describing to Barrow the tricks he had used to render the city indefensible.

Early the next morning, on 1 October, the Australians entered Damascus. The leading elements of the Arab army arrived at about the same time; the 5th Cavalry Division rode in

at 10:30. Within the city's barracks several thousand more Turks passively awaited their captors. Of the entire Yilderim Army Group, perhaps 17,000 men had evaded capture, but of these only 4,000, including the German 146th Regiment, were fighting troops, the rearguard of a disorganised column making its way up the road to Homs; a very few stragglers also passed through Colonel von Oppen's outpost line at Riyaq.

BARADA GORGE, 30 SEPTEMBER 1918

At about 16:30 elements of the Australian Mounted Division, led by the French Régiment Mixte and the 2nd New Zealand Machine Gun Squadron, reached the cliffs on the southern edge of the 100-yard-wide Barada Gorge and opened fire on the thousands of troops, transport vehicles and railway trains below. Two miles to the west the 9th ALH also reached the edge of the gorge and did likewise. The Australians fired and fired till the road was littered with the bodies of men and animals and the wreckage of transport wagons. Four hundred dead were later found on the road, and it took several days to burn the vehicles in order to clear the pass.

On to Aleppo

Allenby's decision to maintain the pursuit to the north was a bold one, given the inflexible rule that the power of an offensive decreases in proportion to the ground it has covered. Casualties apart, many of the Desert Mounted Corps' horses had foundered and been destroyed because of the demands made upon them, and of those that remained the artillery was entitled to claim the fittest. Equally serious was an outbreak of malaria and influenza, contracted from the Turks. During the worst week disease put over 3,000 men in hospital; four times as many deaths resulted from these diseases as had been incurred during the battle itself.

The burden of the pursuit fell on Macandrew's 5th Cavalry Division, which, though the healthiest in the corps, had been reduced by sickness to some 1,500 sabres. To balance the deficiency, Macandrew was given the 2nd, 11th and 12th LAMBs and the 1st, 2nd and 7th LCPs to act as a mechanised advance guard. An RAF squadron was also placed at his disposal.

There was very little fighting. On 6 October Riyaq was taken without opposition and the next day armoured car patrols found that the enemy had also abandoned Beirut. XXI Corps' cavalry regiment and 7th Indian Division occupied the city on 8 October and were ordered to push on to Tripoli, which they reached on 13 October, giving Allenby another supply port.

Meanwhile, Macandrew had reorganised his division into two columns: Column A, consisting of the mechanised units and 15th Cavalry Brigade, possessed the speed, punch and firepower required for deep penetration; Column B, containing the rest of the division, would follow as quickly as possible and go into action as and when needed. In this manner Homs was reached on 16 October and the advance continued down the valley of the Orontes. On 20 October Allenby ordered Macandrew to halt at Hama, but relented when the latter protested that 'there was no opposition worth thinking of at Aleppo' – an assertion confirmed by air reports that the enemy was leaving the city in large numbers.

Lieutenant-general Sir Harry Chauvel, Commanding the Desert Mounted Corps, enters Damascus on 2 October, escorted by men of the 2nd Light Horse and units representing the British, Australian, New Zealand, Indian and French units under his command. (IWM Neg Q12378)

General Allenby arrives at Damascus, 3 October. He is exchanging salutes with recently released Italian prisoners of war, employed by the Turks as labourers. (IWM Neg Q12383)

With an Arab force operating on its right, the advance guard continued northwards, and on 22 October it fought a running battle with a Turkish motor convoy protected by an improvised German armoured car. This machine, heavier and slower than the Rolls-Royce cars, was also handicapped by having solid tyres and was ultimately abandoned by its crew. The Turks were further hindered by two of their own aircraft which joined in the fray on the side of the British. Saragab was taken on 24 October, but the following day Macandrew, whose advance guard was now two days' march ahead of his main body, received a temporary check when Mustapha Kemal rejected a summons to surrender Aleppo. Kemal, however, was bluffing, for he was already preparing to withdraw in the face of Arab pressure from the east and north. On 26 October the armoured cars entered the city, already in Arab hands, while 15th Cavalry Brigade engaged the Turkish rearguard at Haritan. Three days later Muslimiya Junction, through which ran the enemy's rail lifeline to the Mesopotamian front, was also captured.

On their own, the defeats in Palestine and Mesopotamia would very probably have led Turkey to seek terms, but the crushing of her ally Bulgaria the previous month at Vardar had added urgency to the situation and the Grand Vizier had already requested an armistice. This was granted on 31 October.

In the 38 days since the start of the Battle of Megiddo Allenby's troops had destroyed three Turkish armies, advanced 350 miles and captured 76,000 prisoners, 360 guns and 89 locomotives; no accurate figures exist for the numbers of enemy killed and wounded. This victory, as complete as any in history, had been achieved at the cost of only 782 killed, 4,179 wounded and 382 missing.

THE ARAB RAIDS AGAINST THE RAILWAY AND THE MARCH OF THE 4TH CAVALRY DIVISION, 16–29 SEPTEMBER 1918

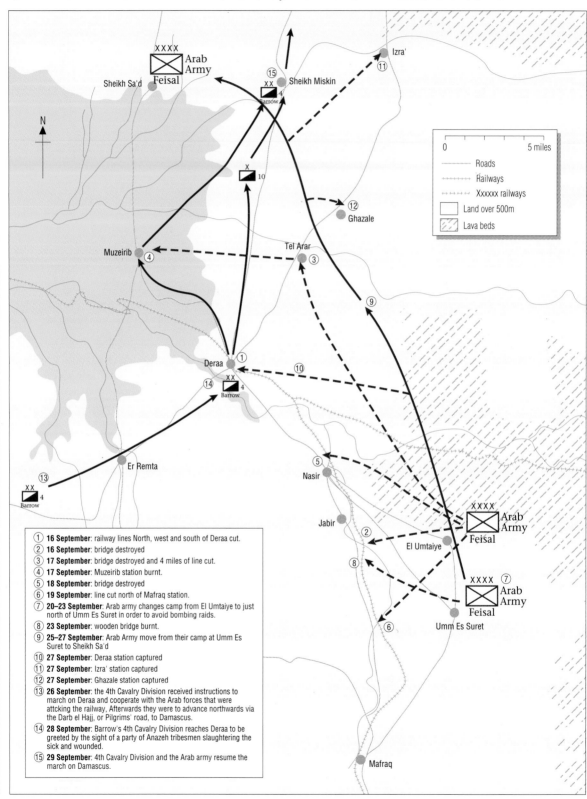

1. **16 September**: railway lines North, west and south of Deraa cut.
2. **16 September**: bridge destroyed
3. **17 September**: bridge destroyed and 4 miles of line cut.
4. **17 September**: Muzeirib station burnt.
5. **18 September**: bridge destroyed
6. **19 September**: line cut north of Mafraq station.
7. **20–23 September**: Arab army changes camp from El Umtaiye to just north of Umm Es Suret in order to avoid bombing raids.
8. **23 September**: wooden bridge burnt.
9. **25–27 September**: Arab Army move from their camp at Umm Es Suret to Sheikh Sa'd
10. **27 September**: Deraa station captured
11. **27 September**: Izra' station captured
12. **27 September**: Ghazale station captured
13. **26 September**: the 4th Cavalry Division received instructions to march on Deraa and cooperate with the Arab forces that were attcking the railway, Afterwards they were to advance northwards via the Darb el Hajj, or Pilgrims' road, to Damascus.
14. **28 September**: Barrow's 4th Cavalry Division reaches Deraa to be greeted by the sight of a party of Anazeh tribesmen slaughtering the sick and wounded.
15. **29 September**: 4th Cavalry Division and the Arab army resume the march on Damascus.

THE PURSUIT FROM DAMASCUS TO ALEPPO, 1–28 OCTOBER 1918

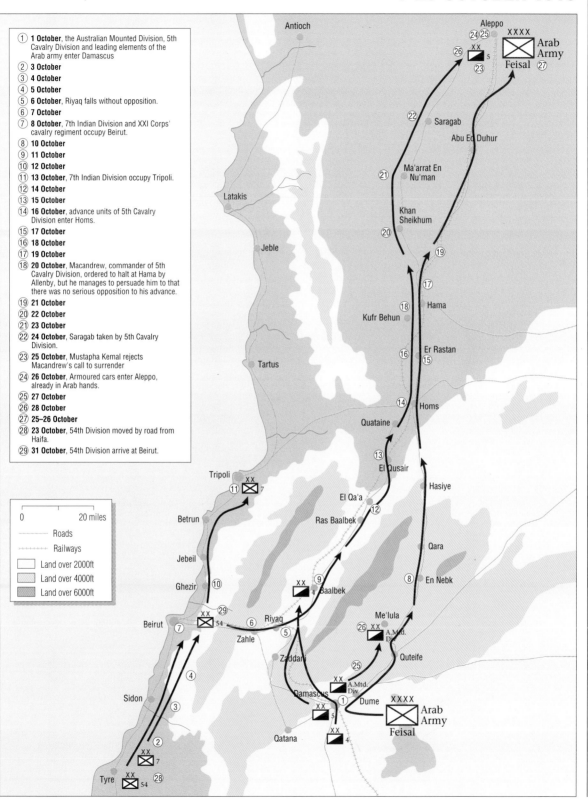

1. **1 October**, the Australian Mounted Division, 5th Cavalry Division and leading elements of the Arab army enter Damascus
2. **3 October**
3. **4 October**
4. **5 October**
5. **6 October**, Riyaq falls without opposition.
6. **7 October**
7. **8 October**, 7th Indian Division and XXI Corps' cavalry regiment occupy Beirut.
8. **10 October**
9. **11 October**
10. **12 October**
11. **13 October**, 7th Indian Division occupy Tripoli.
12. **14 October**
13. **15 October**
14. **16 October**, advance units of 5th Cavalry Division enter Homs.
15. **17 October**
16. **18 October**
17. **19 October**
18. **20 October**, Macandrew, commander of 5th Cavalry Division, ordered to halt at Hama by Allenby, but he manages to persuade him to that there was no serious opposition to his advance.
19. **21 October**
20. **22 October**
21. **23 October**
22. **24 October**, Saragab taken by 5th Cavalry Division.
23. **25 October**, Mustapha Kemal rejects Macandrew's call to surrender
24. **26 October**, Armoured cars enter Aleppo, already in Arab hands.
25. **27 October**
26. **28 October**
27. **25–26 October**
28. **23 October**, 54th Division moved by road from Haifa.
29. **31 October**, 54th Division arrive at Beirut.

0   20 miles

Roads
Railways
Land over 2000ft
Land over 4000ft
Land over 6000ft

THE LEGACY OF MEGIDDO

nitially, the opening phases of the battle were known as the battles of Nablus and Sharon, but as its epicentre rested on El Lajjun (Megiddo), the scene of Pharaoh Thutmosis III's great victory in 1469 BC, it was logical that Allenby's equally decisive victory should take the ancient battlefield's name.

At Megiddo in 1918 all the elements of what became known as the *blitzkrieg* technique were combined for the first time. They included an elaborate deception plan, a holding action by XX Corps, the generation of immense violence at the chosen point of breakthrough, deep penetration, the indirect approach to the objective, the infliction of strategic paralysis, and sustained air support at every level. Equally important was the fact that the critical phase of the battle was fought at the operative, or corps, level. The combined effect of these elements broke the Turkish will to fight during the first hours, for although the average Turk, given a reasonable chance, was a doughty fighter, in these circumstances, battered by superior artillery, confronted by aggressive

The Emir Feisal leaves the Hotel Victoria in Damascus, following a meeting with Allenby. Some of his own regulars can be seen on the right of the picture. (IWM Neg Q12364)

Logistics demands led to one of the campaign's major engineering achievements, namely rendering the famous Ladder of Tyre, where the road consisted of a series of steep rocky shelves, fit for motor vehicles. Three Indian pioneer battalions and two companies of the Egyptian Labour Corps completed the task in two and a half days. (IWM Neg Q12396)

infantry, surrounded by cavalry for whom he had already developed a healthy respect, and bereft of orders from above, it is no wonder that he preferred to surrender as all about him dissolved into chaos; the number of prisoners taken tells its own story.

It does not matter that the primary instrument of Allenby's victory was mounted cavalry rather than armoured formations, although armoured vehicles did play a significant role from time to time. What counted was mobility. Analysis reveals that the Desert Mounted Corps' daily rate of advance between 19 and 21 September was actually twice as fast as that of the German panzer corps during the 1941 invasion of the USSR and the 1944 Allied breakout from the Normandy beachhead, and marginally faster than that of the Israeli armoured divisions during the Six Day War of 1967.

There were similarities to Megiddo in 'Sichelschnitt', the Von Manstein plan which gave Germany victory in the West during the summer of

Solid-tyred, chain-driven motor lorry negotiating the newly completed Ladder of Tyre road, up which it was now possible to tow 60-pdr. guns. (IWM Neg Q12475)

1940, although other thought processes were also present. There were definite echoes of the battle later that year in Operation Compass, which resulted in the destruction of the Italian armies in North Africa, and that is hardly surprising as the British Commander-in-Chief Middle East, General Sir Archibald Wavell, had served under and was a great admirer of Allenby. It is possible to cite numerous similar parallels of which the most recent, Operation Desert Sword, the ground phase of the 1990–1991 Gulf War, bears a striking resemblance to Megiddo.

The immediate aftermath of Allenby's great victory saw the Ottoman Empire stripped of its Arab lands and finally vanish into history. Today's political map of the Middle East bears no relation to that of 1918. There does, however, remain an active reminder of one of the consequences of Megiddo. When the war ended the British and imperial armies had over 22,000 horses serving in the Middle East. It would have been uneconomic to bring them home, even if shipping space was available, which it was not. They were, therefore, sold locally, either for food or work. This was heart-breaking for the troopers who had ridden them, who knew only too well that their new owners would treat them, if not with active cruelty, then with a mixture of ignorance and indifference that would produce hardship. During the early 1930s the Cavalry Division in Egypt was commanded by Major-general G. F. H. Brooke, whose wife, Mrs Dorothy Brooke, was so disgusted by the condition of former British army horses that she founded the Brooke Hospital for Horses in Cairo. The hospital, supported by voluntary donations, is still active today, and provides treatment without charge; furthermore, thanks to its education programme, it is fair to say that the condition of working horses in Egypt is a great deal better than can be found in some areas of the Middle East. Thus it is possible that a tourist whose great-grandfather made the great ride from Jaffa to Aleppo may ride in a *gharri* drawn by a horse descended from that which carried him.

The 2nd Battalion The Black Watch (7th Indian Division) enter Beirut behind their pipers on 10 October, having marched the 96 miles from Haifa in eight days. Note the regimental hackle fixed to the helmets. (IWM Neg Q12407)

THE BATTLEFIELD TODAY

The battlefield of Megiddo lies in northern Israel and the lines of the subsequent pursuit passes through modern Lebanon and Jordan into Syria. To follow events on the ground in chronological order therefore presents obvious difficulties to visitors wishing to leave Israeli territory, and in view of the unsettled state of certain areas a welcome is not necessarily assured. Careful planning in conjunction with the relevant government authority is therefore strongly recommended.

Much of the country is more densely populated than it was at the time of the battle. Agriculture, too, has been more intensively developed. There are fewer railways but many more good roads. I am indebted to Lieutenant-colonel David Eshel IDF (Rtd.) for the following description of the critical terrain at the time of writing.

'Although the main attraction of Tel Megiddo today is an impressive archaeological site, the top of the hill provides a superb observation point, overlooking the scene of events on 20 September 1918, when the Desert Mounted Corps, emerging from the Musmus Pass, now Wadi Yiron, chased the Turks across the plain to the Jezreel valley.

2nd Battalion the Leicestershire Regiment (also 7th Indian Division) in their brigade bivouac near Beirut. (IWM Neg Q12420)

'The visitor can follow the advance of 4th Cavalry Division through the length of the Musmus Pass. Starting at Hadera on the coast, drive along a modern four-lane highway passing the water points at Ara village, and on up to El Lajjun. Here a kibbutz named Megiddo is situated. Nearby, to the north-west, is a hill named Yoshya, which also provides an excellent panorama. Megiddo Junction is at the exit from the Musmus Pass. Turn left towards Haifa and after driving half a kilometre turn left again to visit the archaeological site and the summit of the Tel, from which Afula (now Affule), Liman von Sanders' communications centre, can be seen. This is now a thriving township and has completely changed, although it is possible to see the ruins of the old railway station and some derelict buildings if one turns left at the central roundabout. Returning to Megiddo Junction, turn east and follow the route of 3rd Light Horse Brigade towards Jenin, within which is a monument to German airmen killed while serving with Yilderim. However, for security reasons, access to the town might be prohibited.

'To the north-west, about three kilometres' drive along the Haifa road, one reaches Kibbutz Mishmar Haemek, at the exit from the Abu Shushe Pass, now Wadi Millek, through which the 5th Cavalry Division rode. Starting again from Hadera, drive along the old Haifa road to Furaides Junction, then turn east as far as Yokneam Junction, which is at

British and French vessels in Beirut harbour. Piles of ballast, sleepers and rails have been landed so that the quay can be connected to the main railway system. Unfortunately, sections of the steep Beirut – Damascus line used a rack-and-pinion system for which too few suitable locomotives were available and the infantry's advance continued to Tripoli. (IWM Neg Q12397)

the exit from the pass. From the high ground it is possible to look across the Jezreel valley to Nazareth, on the ridge to the north. This is the route 5th Cavalry Division took to reach Nazareth, in which the old building housing the Yilderim General Headquarters still exist.

'The modern visitor cannot expect to see many relics of the battle, although the topography is unchanged and little imagination is required to trace the course of events.

'However, twice in more recent times Megiddo became a battleground once again. During the 1948 war, units from the newly created Golani Infantry Brigade captured the Tel from an Iraqi volunteer force under Fawzi el Kaukaji after a sharp battle. From the Lajun police fort near the junction, the Iraqis counter-attacked with the support of armoured cars. The Golani troops stood their ground and, crossing the open fields at night, blew breaches in the walls of the fort with demolition charges and, after furious close-quarter fighting, captured it. The fort is now a high-security prison. In the 1967 war the Junction also witnessed the beginning of the attack by Moshe Brill's 45th Mechanised Brigade against strong positions held by the Jordanian 25th Infantry Brigade on the hills overlooking Megiddo, from which the Jordanians were shelling the Ramat David Airbase in the Jezreel valley with 155mm Long Toms.'

Tripoli was taken on 13 October. Here a camel transport convoy is seen assembling on the outskirts of the city. (IWM Neg Q12428)

CHRONOLOGY

1914

29 October The Ottoman Empire declares war on the Allies.

1915

14 January – 3 February Turkish assault on the Suez Canal repulsed; Turks withdraw to Beersheba.

1916

January – July The British, under General Sir Archibald Murray, advance slowly across the Sinai, methodically extending their logistic support facilities as they go; in the Western Desert the Turkish-backed Senussi invasion of Egypt is checked; start of the British-supported Arab revolt against the Turks in the Hejaz.

3 August Battle of Romani. Turkish counter-attack on the British rail-head in Sinai repulsed with heavy losses.

December The British reach El Arish.

1917

8–9 January Battle of Magruntein; Sinai cleared of last Turkish forces.

26 March First Battle of Gaza; British attack fails to capture the town; Turks establish Gaza/Beersheba line.

17–19 April Second Battle of Gaza; further attempt to break the Gaza/Beersheba line fails; Murray replaced by General Sir Edmund Allenby.

31 October Third Battle of Gaza; Allenby turns the Turkish flank at Beersheba and breaks through at Gaza; Turks evacuate Gaza and withdraw.

13–14 November Battle of Junction Station; further Turkish reverse, followed by fighting in the Judean hills.

9 December Allenby captures Jerusalem.

1918

January – September Arab revolt in the Hejaz continues, pinning down Turkish troops; the demands of other theatres of war prevent Allenby from launching the decisive offensive until the autumn.

26–31 March First raid against Amman.

30 April – 3 May Second raid against Amman.

19 September Battle of Megiddo begins; Turkish XXII Corps destroyed; breakout of Desert Mounted Corps; capture of Tul Karm.

Night 19/20 September Musmus Pass secured.

20 September El Lajjun (Megiddo), Afula, Beisan and Jenin taken; Nazareth attacked.

On 25 October Major-general Macandrew, GOC 5th Cavalry Division, despatched Captain Macintyre of the 7th Light Car Patrol under a flag of truce to demand the surrender of Aleppo. Mustapha Kemal, the garrison commander, rejected the demand but was already planning to withdraw that night. (IWM Neg Q12450)

Night 20/21 September Bridge at Jisr el Majami secured.

21 September Much of Turkish Seventh Army destroyed by air attack in the Wadi Far'a; Nazareth taken.

22 September Jisr el Damiya ford captured by Chaytor's force.

23 September Haifa and Acre taken; remaining Jordan fords closed; Es Salt taken.

25 September Samakh stormed; Amman captured; Arabs intensify attacks on the Hejaz railway.

26 September Engagement at Irbid.

27 September Engagements at El Remte and Jisr Benat Yakub; Deraa falls to Arabs; Turkish II Corps surrenders to Chaytor's force south of Amman.

28 September Kuneitra taken; 4th Cavalry Division reaches Deraa.

29 September Engagement at Sa'sa.

30 September Engagements at Kau Kab and Kiswe; much of Turkish Fourth Army destroyed in the Barada Gorge.

1 October Desert Mounted Corps and Arabs enter Damascus.

6 October Riyaq taken.

8 October Beirut taken.

13 October Tripoli taken.

16 October Homs taken.

26 October Engagement at Haritan; 5th Cavalry Division and Arabs enter Aleppo.

29 October Muslimiya Junction captured.

31 October Ottoman Empire granted armistice.

WARGAMING MEGIDDO

Given that the fighting spread across many hundreds of square miles, it would be very difficult indeed to reproduce it in its entirety on the games table. It would, of course, be possible to replay the entire battle at the strategic or operative levels using any of the hexagonal map methods in conjunction with unit symbols, but unless the facts of history are tampered with, the result is unlikely to be very different. A larger, well-managed army employing mobility as the decisive weapon is unlikely to lose to a smaller, indifferently administered army with inferior mobility. At the tactical level, however, the result is not necessarily a foregone conclusion. At Nazareth, for example, the attacking commander was over-cautious, failed in his primary task because of it, and lost his job; at Irbid, the commanding officer concerned was over-confident and was lucky not only to escape with comparatively few casualties, but also to retain his command. There were also a number of situations which, while they might not have influenced the eventual outcome of the battle, could have presented the

Sherifian troops enter Aleppo early on the morning of 26 October. (IWM Neg Q12439)

12th LAMB entered Aleppo the same day, parking their armoured cars in the shade provided by the canopy of the now deserted railway station. (IWM Neg Q12440)

victors with worrying local situations and imposed delay when it was needed least. What if, for example, the Turks had displayed a little more energy and taken possession of the Musmus Pass before the vanguard of the 4th Cavalry Division arrived?

Further reasons for adopting the tactical level include the ability to duplicate local terrain and employ appropriate scale figures and equipment to regenerate the feel of the engagement. Rules should be fairly simple, along the lines of those set out in the books of Donald Featherstone, Bruce Quarrie and Terence Wise.

It is, however, worth making a number of additional points that relate specifically to this campaign. Allenby achieved complete surprise at every level, and some allowance must be made for this. Again, following the spectacular charges of 1917 – Beersheba, Huj and El Mughar – the Turks were very much in awe of the Desert Mounted Corps. Curiously, although the Asia Korps was to distinguish itself in its later actions, many Germans did not fight well during the first days of the battle, being as shaken as their allies by the catastrophe that had overtaken them. In contrast, once the breakthrough had been achieved, the Desert Mounted Corps was at the top of its form, knowing that the enemy had been dealt a mortal blow; only the condition of its horses and, latterly, sickness, could slow it down.

Beyond the original front line, little or no barbed wire was encountered but, as we have seen, there were plenty of physical obstacles including steep hills, boulder fields, lava beds and, at the Kishon river, quicksand that could swallow horse and man. Another factor which should be taken into account is the need to water horses. Water was not the serious problem it had been in earlier years, but if the facilities were poor, the process could cost irrecoverable time, as at the Musmus Pass.

The Desert Mounted Corps used the sword or lance during mounted charges and the rifle and bayonet for its dismounted attacks. Almost all charges were pressed home because the Turks did not adjust the elevation of their machine guns beyond that required to engage infantry targets. Horses were hit in the legs, quarters and chest, but even mortally wounded horses often completed a charge. This was evidently not a mistake made by the German defenders of Samakh. During dismounted attacks an approach in dead ground was used whenever possible. Horse-holders would be told off before the assault went in, the effect being to reduce the strength of the attacking force by between one-sixth and one-tenth. All attacks, including those delivered straight off the line of march, were delivered with fire support from the unit's own machine guns. Where necessary, these would be supplemented by the brigade machine gun squadron and RHA batteries. Armoured cars were used in the deep reconnaissance and advance to contact roles and in appropriate circumstances could supply close fire support. They were, of course, vulnerable to artillery and there were areas where the terrain inhibited their use off the road. The Turks did possess a few German armoured cars, mainly over-large, heavy and slow Erhardts, but little use seems to have been made of them; some are known to have been fitted with flanged wheels and used to patrol the Hejaz railway.

Even if one departs from the established script, there is plenty of scope for the tactical wargame. Scenarios can include the narrow-gauge railway system, villages, armoured cars and aircraft; the desert, mountain passes or the Jordan fords; the only parameters are the need to maintain historical accuracy and the extent of the players' imagination. Wargaming aspects of Megiddo, the last great cavalry victory, can be both stimulating and challenging fought at the operative or corps level.

On 27 October 12th LAMB began probing northwards from Aleppo towards Muslimiya Junction. (IWM Neg Q12447)

FURTHER READING

The most complete record of the campaign is contained in *The History of the Great War – Military Operations Egypt & Palestine Part II*, the Official History, by Cyril Falls, published by HMSO in 1930. Falls also updated the story in a condensed but very readable account, *Armageddon 1918*, (Weidenfeld & Nicolson 1964). Also recommended is the future Field Marshal Earl Wavell's *The Palestine Campaign*, 1931.

The operations of the Desert Mounted Corps have been meticulously researched and recorded by the Marquess of Anglesey in his *History of British Cavalry Vol 5: 1914-1919 Egypt, Palestine and Syria*, (Leo Cooper 1994). The relevant British, Australian, New Zealand and Indian regimental histories also repay study, but are now rarely encountered outside libraries and archives.

Details of the hardware employed can be found in *Military Small Arms of the 20th Century* by Ian Hogg and John Weeks, (Arms & Armour Press 1991); *The Illustrated Encyclopaedia of Artillery* by Ian Hogg, (Quarto 1987); and *War Cars – British Armoured Cars in the First World War* by David Fletcher, (HMSO 1987).

Recommended biographies include Wavell's *Allenby – A Study in Greatness* (1940) and A. J. Hill's *Chauvel of the Light Horse* (1978). Much interesting autobiographical comment can be found in General George Barrow's *The Fire of Life* (1942) and General Liman von Sanders' *Five Years in Turkey* (Annapolis 1927).

INDEX

REVERE PUBLIC LIBRARY

3 6661 00102 2018

DISCARDED

DATE DUE

GAYLORD   PRINTED IN U.S.A.